D0502183

DATE DUE

How Christians Grow

HOW
CHRISTIANS
GROW

RUSSELL T. HITT

New York   Oxford
OXFORD UNIVERSITY PRESS
1979

Copyright © 1979 by Oxford University Press, Inc.

Library of Congress Cataloging in Publication Data

Hitt, Russell T.
  How Christians grow.
  Bibliography: p.
  1. Christian life—1960-   I. Title.
BV4501.2.H524   248′.4   79-2261
ISBN 0-19-502558-X

Second printing, 1979

Printed in the United States of America

To David and Susan

Preface

J. B. Phillips in his literate, contemporary translation of the New Testament uses the expression "spiritually adult" in rendering Philippians 3:15. To be spiritually adult seems a reasonable goal for the Christian today.

This may seem too big an order for the pilgrim beset by many contrary forces. Certainly our world burdens us with complex and seemingly insoluble issues that leave us gasping and confused. The world seems to be "squeezing us into its mold," to use another expression from Phillips. Rather than having any ambitions for spiritual adulthood, we seek only to cope with life's unrelenting pressures.

In earlier days devout men longed to experience the beatific vision, a rapturous union with God himself. "Blessed are the pure in heart, for they shall see God," our Lord taught.

Writing of his own journey in faith, St. Paul declares: "I do not consider myself to have 'arrived' spiritually, nor do I consider myself already perfect. But I keep going on, grasping ever more firmly that purpose for which Christ Jesus grasped me. My brothers, I do not consider myself to have fully grasped it even now. But I do concentrate on this: I leave the past behind and with hands outstretched to whatever lies ahead I go straight for the goal—my reward the honor of my high calling by God in Christ Jesus" (Philippians 3:12–14).[1]

1. J. B. Phillips, *The New Testament in Modern English*, New York: Macmillan, 1959.

Do not reply that Paul possessed a special dynamic for growth that is not available to all Christian believers today. He too was aware of the pressures and temptations of a secularistic culture. Speaking of "the enemies of the cross of Christ"—those who have no vision of God and no interest in spiritual growth for themselves or others—he declares: "These men are heading for utter destruction—their god is their own appetite; their pride is in what they should be ashamed of; and this world is the limit of their horizon" (Philippians 3:19).[2]

Dietrich Bonhoeffer asked the questions, "What did Jesus mean to say to us? What is his will for us today? How can he help us to be good Christians in the modern world?"[3]

There is much talk currently about church renewal, and that is a valid issue. But more to the point is the need for individual Christians to be renewed. Such a renaissance starts with a renewal of personal devotion to Jesus Christ. This is not to belittle concern for biblical orthodoxy, proper modes of worship, or social involvement. But Jesus Christ is for each of us personally both our beginning and our goal—our Alpha and Omega. As we "grasp" the purpose for which Christ has "grasped" us, the scales will drop from our eyes and we will see fresh and glorious vistas before us. If, like St. Paul, we press forward, we will grow towards spiritual maturity. And the beatific vision can be ours.

R.T.H.

Merion Station, Pa.
March 1979

2. J. B. Phillips, *The New Testament in Modern English*, New York: Macmillan, 1959.

3. Dietrich Bonhoeffer, *The Cost of Discipleship*, London: Student Christian Movement Press, 1948.

Acknowledgments

I sought to pick the brains of a lot of worthy people as the concept of this book developed. Even though I may impress the reader with some big names, none of these scholars and friends can be blamed for what I have written. But I am grateful for their help.

They include Dr. W. Fred Graham of Justin S. Morrill College, Michigan State University; Dr. Richard Lovelace, professor of Church History at Gordon-Conwell Theological Seminary; Dr. Norman H. Maring, former dean of the faculty, Eastern Baptist Theological Seminary; and Dr. Bernard L. Ramm, recently a professor of theology at Eastern; Colin K. Becroft, a long-time confidant and associate in the work of Scripture Union; Robert T. Coote, my former *Eternity* colleague; Jennie Pierce; and the Rev. Robert S. Williamson, my pastor at the Presbyterian Church of the Covenant, Bala-Cynwyd, Pennsylvania. There are many more whose names will go unheralded though they know how grateful I am for their suggestions.

My special thanks to Stephen Board, who reviewed the manuscript and saved me from many literary and theological gaucheries.

Finally, I must publicly acknowledge my co-author and yokefellow, Lillian, who besides serving as chauffeur, errand girl, researcher, buffer, secretary, and typist, is my beloved wife. In the frenetic last moments, she proved her continued ability to produce an inerrant typescript.

R.T.H.

Contents

How Christians Grow

1

It's Not an Empty Promise

My new friend, an Italian contractor building a house across the road from us, and I were discussing the general state of world affairs. We moaned and groaned about inflation, taxes, crooked politicians, and the sheer frustration of trying to get anything done.

Inevitably the conversation turned to the deteriorating moral tone of our society. Francesco waved his hands in despair and blurted out: "The whole world is going to hell."

I told him I was engaged in writing a book about the possibility for people of our generation to live triumphantly in spite of all the obstacles that seem to stand in our way. Although I did not make any grandiose promises, I suggested that the Christian way offered release from our common frustration and despair.

Francesco encouraged me to continue my writing. He returned to his construction work.

I would not be honest if I did not confess that to write on the subject of Christian growth seemed at first to be a formidable task. Yet as I progressed I realized that I was discovering something that should be shared with other Christians and men of goodwill.

I also discovered a host of those who long years ago pursued "the beatific vision"—Benedict, Ignatius Loyola, Francis de Sales, Theresa of Avila, John of the Cross, and many more. I became acquainted with many who dedicated their lives to Christ and a life of humble service to men.

At first I wondered what I could say that the sages and saints have not discovered in their personal anguish and suffering.

My task, I found, was to get back to primary sources, seeking to avoid the unbiblical accretions of tradition and the distortions of cultic mentalities.

The secondary sources were often dreary, poorly written books dealing with sanctification, the path of holiness, and the grim subject of crucifixion. Yet I also came across treasured authors like Helmut Thielicke, Dietrich Bonhoeffer, C. S. Lewis, Lesslie Newbigin, and Ronald Knox plus some very stimulating new ones like Donald Bloesch and Lewis Smedes.

I am an evangelical Protestant affiliated with one of the major denominations, but I soon learned that Roman Catholics have written more extensively in the area of what is called spirituality. Their books demonstrate a deep devotion to Christ and an intense desire to serve God through self-discipline and service to mankind.

Protestants in the liberal tradition have been concerned about social action. Evangelical Protestants stress what we should believe. Proper doctrine rates high. But neither of these divided streams of Protestantism have stressed the importance of what we *are*. Well-rounded Christianity, of course, must embrace what we *are* through relationship to Christ, what we believe, and what we are doing about translating creed into loving service.

I am active enough as a churchman to know that most professing Christians are dissatisfied with their lives and far too many are distressed by the dullness of our congregational life. All Christians, without exception, face serious personal problems—domestic discord, children out of fellowship with the family, financial burdens—the list is endless. Each of us is looking for help, some seek it desperately. My hope is that this little volume may provide some guidance.

Recently a new force of younger believers has joined the household of faith. They are full of exuberance and life, and they want to be effective as witnesses and servants. They feel thwarted by the religious status quo and frustrated by what seems to them an impotent and unresponsive church.

Throngs of professing Christians attend services regularly. The cushions in the pews where they sit are well worn. But there is little evidence that they are excited about being Christians. They do not appear to have aspirations for growth. One longs to share the good word that the grace of God can change them and enable them to reach new heights of joy and fulfillment.

Yet no matter how one approaches the subject of spirituality, one is sure to meet with contrary reactions and vigorous dissent. For the saints are never more "righteous" than when we challenge their pet spiritual convictions—whether they are right or wrong.

From the start I wanted this to be a book that would be helpful to Christians of varying traditions of worship, theology, and life style. This creates the possibility of not communicating successfully to anyone at all. We all have our own way of expressing "the truth." Most of us act as if our position on any subject is the inerrant Word of God transmitted directly to us.

Even the reputedly genial Simeon Stylites, who perched on a stone column in Syria for thirty-seven years in penitential discipline might question any challenge to his method of attaining holiness. He had a reputation for being sweet tempered. Yet I fear that he might react unfavorably to the suggestion that removing one's self from the world might not be the best course of action—or inaction. After all, he was the one who led the tradition of six centuries of pillar hermits!

But we must not mock the monastic tradition. Through the long centuries the ascetics have produced a treasury of literature on spirituality. Of that we will say more later.

Think too of the long procession of bleeding flagellants who have sought to appease God's wrath and achieve personal holiness through flogging themselves or even enduring simulated crucifixion. Can you imagine the frustration and disbelief of these zealots if you were to tell them that their self-atonement was in vain, that another had borne the pain and suffering for all their sins?

It seems easy to deal with Simeon Stylites and the flagellants. They are so distant in time and theological tradition from most of us. We can rather smugly express our compassion for them in their failure to comprehend the grace of God. Yet do we not stand on the pillars of our own pride and self-righteousness and look down with patronizing pity at the benighted failures all around us? "God, I thank thee, that I am not as other men." Yes, most of us possess the spirit of the Pharisee rather than the publican.

I was once talking to an elder of the United Presbyterian Church, who ranted against the preachers of his denomination. In his simplistic analysis, all the evils of the church stemmed from inept clerics. I did not discern even a hint of self-reproach or personal repentance in his appraisal of the problems of his communion.

Or consider the Fundamentalist who has attained the heights of perfection but finds no good in the charismatic believer. On the other hand, many Pentecostals and charismatics seem to impose second-class citizenship in the Kingdom on those who have not received "the baptism."

To discover the dynamics of Christian growth one must

sort through a myriad of conflicting claims and uproot as heresies preciously held beliefs. It is an awesome task.

Consider some of the deeply ingrained errors that seem to appear in new forms in every generation:

1. *Our good works save us or somehow help in achieving our salvation.* Someone has pointed out that there are basically only two religions in the world: (a) one that enables man to attain salvation or perfection by his own efforts and (b) the true religion which offers salvation only by the grace of God.

"For by grace are ye saved through faith; and that not of yourselves: it is the gift of God: Not of works, lest any man should boast" (Ephesians 2:8, 9).

Of course, good works are desirable, indeed mandatory, for those who profess to be united to Jesus Christ. These works flow from the new life in Christ. But to see "works" as a means of obtaining that new life in Christ is utterly wrong.

2. *There is something inherently evil about the body.* Even some of the most illustrious Fathers of the church accepted the error, which is found in the teaching of Plato, that the body is inferior to the soul. This concept went so far that some Neoplatonists could not accept the reality of Incarnation. True Christianity never teaches that the body is evil or "the prison of the soul."

Many forms of asceticism developed from this false concept, as did perhaps the prudery of Victorianism and the legalistic codes of some contemporary Christianity. Even worthies like John Bunyan, who was conscience-stricken because he enjoyed the pealing of the church bells, and David Brainerd, who spent most of his brief life in self-castigation, were subtly lured away from the inexpressible joy which should be the heritage of every believer.

3. *The tendency to express Christian life by means of a legalistic code.* St. Paul forthrightly confronted St. Peter for

siding with the Jerusalem party in the infant church. The Judaizers insisted that Gentile converts must be circumcised as a prerequisite of salvation. St. Paul denounced this effort to bring the new believers into a yoke of bondage instead of liberation in Christ.

Legalism still continues to harass the people of God, seeking to impose a man-made superstructure of do's and don'ts as a guide to proper Christian conduct. St. Paul declares (Galatians 3:23–4:7) that the principle of law-keeping militates against spiritual maturity. These erroneous and distorted concepts of the means to Christian growth seem to thrive as much within the household of faith as without.

Why is there a need for another book on Christian growth? Why is the subject worth discussing? And who is arrogant enough to feel he has anything new to add to the discussion?

The author has been involved in Christian activity most of his adult life. Reared in a conservative Christian home, he has had opportunity to develop the friendship of a number of Christians, leaders as well as followers. All too few of them seemed to show much evidence of growth toward spiritual maturity. Few seemed to find the happy secret of growth in Christ. No particular communion, no particular theological emphasis seems to produce the greatest number of maturing believers.

As editor of *Eternity* magazine, which largely deals with contemporary issues in the light of Scripture, the writer has often read letters from readers which indicated a desire to live the more abundant life and to find ways of coping with the contradictions of our existence. How often one has been aware of the inadequacy of our words and intentions.

Cardinal Newman declared that "growth is the only evidence of life." Can there be spiritual growth, if there has not first been a spiritual birth?

Questions tumble over one another:

Why should Christians grow?

Is growth a conscious or unconscious process?

Is growth in plants or animals analogous to growth in human beings? "Consider the lilies of the field, how they grow; they toil not, neither do they spin" (Matthew 6:28).

Is spiritual growth comparable to the physical growth of human beings?

Is growth a steady or intermittent process?

Is growth another way of saying maturing?

Is there danger in being too introspective about our growth? Should one always be taking his own spiritual temperature?

What is the measuring stick of growth?

Can one "grow in grace" in "the present evil world"? Should one close himself off from "the world"?

What inhibiting forces prevent spiritual growth?

Does a growing Christian always have to contend with the likelihood of sin? Is there an escape?

What are the means of growth?

These are some of the questions that we shall face but there will not be any glib answers or formulas. However, there is no reason for any of us to give up the struggle. The Lord himself has urged us to grow. It is worth the effort to seek the way toward spiritual maturity. *It is within our reach!*

2

First, the Diagnosis!

Some years ago my wife and I had as our house guest for several days Dr. Ferenc Kiss, a distinguished Christian physician from Budapest. Taking advantage of our guest's professional knowledge, we consulted him about a physical problem that was troubling a member of the family. While he was interviewing us, we both offered curbstone advice as to how to treat the illness. Neither of us will ever forget the vehement reaction of our doctor friend, who shouted, *"First, the diagnosis!"*

In similar fashion, we must diagnose our spiritual malady before we can proceed with the needed therapy.

We have already been made aware of the fact that growth is the preponderant evidence of life. So we must first explore what we mean by life. This is not physical life, but spiritual life—new life in Christ.

Nicodemus learned from our Lord firsthand that there is an analogy between physical and spiritual life. One has to be born before there can be life. This is true, Jesus tells all of us, both in the physical and spiritual realm. It is not fanatical to speak of being "born again." Rebirth is a basic requirement, as has been revealed to us by the best of authorities.

Quite honestly, the church does not speak with one voice on the details of how we are born spiritually. A large segment teaches that regeneration (that is the theological term for new birth) occurs at the time a child is baptized. Another group of Christians insists that an individual only becomes a Christian when he consciously and publicly acknowledges Jesus Christ as Lord and Savior. There are other views as well, including the vague idea that we become Christians because we are a part of a Christian family or a Christian nation. There is even the belief that all people have received new life because of Christ's perfect redemption. This is called universalism.

So before we get into the subject of Christian growth at all we are enmeshed in theological controversy. We cannot resolve all the issues of religious history but we must realize that there are different ways of approaching the subject. For example, virtually all Christians teach that the rite of baptism identifies an individual with Jesus Christ and his church. No matter what our tradition, we would agree that there is a close relationship between new birth and the initiatory rite of baptism. But we shall not here attempt to resolve the issue of believers' versus infant baptism.

Instead, let us turn to Holy Scripture for light. I think that we can come to agreement on certain basics. It is obvious that Christianity involves Jesus Christ. It is even proper to say that Christianity *is* Christ. There is no room for discussion if we do not agree that Christianity is built on the person and work of Jesus Christ. The merit of Christ's sacrificial death rests upon his deity.

John R. W. Scott, rector emeritus of All Souls' (Anglican) Church in London, believes that there is a threefold line of evidence in Scripture which points to Christ's deity: (1) the claims he made, (2) the character he displayed, and (3) his resurrection from the dead.[1]

1. John R.W. Stott, *Basic Christianity*, Downers Grove, Ill.: Inter-Varsity Press, 1958.

This is the one who dared to say, "I am the way, and the truth, and the life; no one comes to the Father, but by me" (John 14:6 RSV). Another time he boldly declared, "I and the Father are one" (John 10:30 RSV). He bolstered these claims with acts and words that stressed his divinity: He claimed to forgive sins; he offered himself as life; he taught the truth with authority; and he predicted that one day he would judge the world. These verbal declarations were augmented by signs and wonders: changing water into wine, feeding the five thousand, restoring sight to the blind, and raising the dead.

It was Jesus Christ, God's unique Son, who declared, "I am the resurrection and the life; he who believes in me, though he die, yet shall he live, and whoever lives and believes in me shall never die" (John 11:25, 26 RSV).

The ancient prophets of Israel thought that God would deliver his people by a Messiah (Christ) who would be their Deliverer and King. In other prophecies it was indicated that the Messiah would come as a lowly figure, virgin born, and as a suffering servant. He would be Immanuel ("God with us"), God in the flesh, sharing our humanity.

This belief that God took on human flesh in the person of his Son is the cornerstone of our faith, and the Incarnation of God in Christ is the subject of countless anthems and carols. Jesus Christ, who is our Rescuer, Redeemer, and Savior, is not a remote, aloof and unseen God. Rather he identified himself with our humanity, except for our sinful nature.

This chapter deals with first obtaining spiritual life so that we may then know how to take the steps of growth. Jesus says we must be born anew since sin has separated us from our original estate of living fellowship with God. That is why we need a Savior to cleanse us from our sins. "For all have sinned, and come short of the glory of God" (Romans 3:23).

This all may seem a bit confusing. But can we not admit

that we are sinners, that we lack the inner perfection of our own ideals? We lack both the motivation and dynamic of living a commendable life. Of course, we can rationalize and say, "I'm as good as most people I know and better than a lot more." But that only dodges the issue.

Behind the facade of our respectability, we know that we are guilty of greed and jealousy, anger and pride. These are the socially accepted sins which we seldom face realistically. Instead we tend to criticize others for their failures and rationalize our own irresponsible conduct.

As the Lord Jesus points out vividly in the Sermon on the Mount, sin originates in the heart before it erupts in adultery or murder. All of us can recognize blatant anti-social conduct. It is more difficult to deal with the unseen machinations of our complex hearts.

Because of certain psychiatric theories, our culture tends to regard our sins as emotional disorders. Even Christians of deep commitment now talk about our infirmities in psychological terms. It is true, of course, that modern man is plagued by emotional ills. Yet the true situation is almost forgotten today: man is suffering from a deep sickness of the soul.

The great Physician gives us this diagnosis in Matthew 15:19, 20: "For out of the heart proceed evil thoughts, murders, adulteries, fornications, thefts, false witness, blasphemies: These are the things which defile a man. . . ."

Needless to say he is employing "heart" here as a figure of speech. He is not speaking of our blood pump. He is speaking about the center of our inner personal life. The heart is "the source of motives, the seat of passions, the center of thought processes, the spring of conscience." In psychological terms the heart is the cognitive, affective, and volitional center of our being.

The Scriptures teach that man, made in the image of God, no longer reflects divine characteristics. He is out of tune with God's order and perfection. Indeed it is more than being out of tune. The Bible indicates that man is a rebel and a transgressor of God's holy law.

The late Donald Grey Barnhouse, noted Presbyterian expositor, used to say, "You are a sinner if you are less perfect that God." I think each of us must admit we are deceiving ourselves about our professed inherent goodness. The Bible teaches clearly that mankind is spiritually and morally bankrupt.

Otherwise why do we need a Savior?

Relatively speaking we may rate pretty well in this wicked world. But we fool ourselves if we dodge the issue of sin. Being a sinner is part of belonging to the human race.

Sin, which alienates us from God and our fellow men, is the bad news. But the good news (that is what "gospel" means) is that reconciliation with God is freely offered to all men.

St. Paul cried out as he realized his own sinful predicament: "Miserable creature that I am, who is there to rescue me out of this body doomed to death?" Then he answered his own question: "God alone, through Jesus Christ our Lord!" (Romans 7:24-25 NEB).

In another passage St. Paul expands on the concept of our reconciliation to God: "He has reconciled us men to himself through Christ . . . What I mean is, that God was in Christ reconciling the world to himself, no longer holding men's misdeeds against them . . ." (2 Corinthians 5: 18, 19 NEB).

I was once talking to a woman who had just experienced this reconciliation.

"I've been given a new start," she almost shouted in newfound joy.

At this juncture many would say, "I believe Jesus Christ is God's Son and that he died on the Cross, for my sins. Yes, I admit I'm a sinner. But how do I appropriate forgiveness and reconciliation for myself?"

The answer is contained in two short verses in Ephesians (2:8, 9): "For by grace are ye saved through faith; and that not of yourselves: it is the gift of God: Not of works, lest any man should boast."

There are two commonly used words in the religious vocabulary which most people do not fully comprehend—*grace* and *faith*. They are deceivingly short words and the writer struggled for years to understand them.

It is important to realize that God is the initiator in the reconciliation process. Motivated by love that is beyond our capacity to understand, God planned the entire salvage operation of reconciling sinners to himself.

One of the commonest definitions of "grace" is "unmerited favor." It is true that God's extension of his divine favor is undeserved by any of us. There is no inherent goodness in us as human beings that compels God to do something.

"But 'grace,' as used in this context means much more. It is the power emanating from God that gives us strength and empowerment. It is the voice of God that arouses, that awakens, that causes a man to think and inquire."[2]

Salvation and all that is involved in our partaking of it is initiated by God, who freely bestows it. If sin has operated within us to prevent us from union with God, grace is the powerful counterforce that enables us to share in all the benefits of divine redemptive love.

Grace is God coming down to us. Initiated by his love, grace is the spiritual force that invades our lives. Indeed, it is God himself offering us his spiritual favor. He meets us where we are—while we are yet sinners. Salvation is beneficent on his part, unmerited on ours. It is totally God's work, and in love he bestows it on us.

Now for our part: Faith is our response to God, involving

2. C. Brown, *St. Paul's Epistle to the Ephesians: A Devotional Commentary,* 1911.

our minds, our hearts, and our wills. It includes but is much more than mental assent to a propositional statement.

"Faith," in the biblical sense, means turning to God in our need and helplessness, and responding by accepting the gifts he offers. This is more than an abstraction. It means we receive, or trust in, the Lord himself!

"If you confess with your lips that Jesus is Lord and believe in your heart that God raised him from the dead, you will be saved" (Romans 10:9 RSV).

In other words, you demonstrate that you have placed your trust in Jesus Christ by declaring openly (confessing) that you submit to his lordship. That means you acknowledge the supreme honor to which God has exalted him. This is a personal transaction with the divine Savior, who is our only Mediator.

God the Father has given Jesus Christ the title of Lord and he bears the "name which is above every name."

When you call Jesus Christ "Lord," you are recognizing both his deity and authority, and also that you submit to his rule in your life. You are saying, "I am no longer going to run my life. I am henceforth committing myself—my heart, my will, my life to Jesus Christ."

Thus all of your being is involved in this act of commitment. It is important that we see that it is something more than a private devotional exercise. Your commitment is to a real historic person who lived in our world. That is the reason that if you "believe in your heart that God raised him from the dead, you will be saved."

Your experience of commitment is more than subjective. Your faith is placed in the objective and historical reality of Jesus Christ, who penetrated our time-space world and shared our humanity. His death for our sins—he came into the world for this express purpose—and his resurrection are attested facts. "Christ Jesus came into the world to save sinners" (1 Timothy 1:15).

You have to understand that the entire work of redemption was initiated and carried out by God through Jesus Christ his Son and our Lord.

Our response of faith also has an obverse aspect called repentance. As our heart goes out to accept Christ positively, there must be the concomitant decision to turn away from sin. This turning from sin, the basic aspect of repentance, is accompanied by "godly sorrow." "For godly sorrow worketh repentance to salvation . . ." (2 Corinthians 7:10). It must be understood that faith and repentance are two sides of one coin and both operate concurrently. There is no use wasting time asking which comes first, faith or repentance.

At the risk of belaboring the obvious, I want to explain more fully what happens when a person becomes a Christian.

1. *Forgiveness of sin.* Without any striving on your part—only the response of faith, no matter how faltering—you are assured of forgiveness of all your sins. Our Lord bore "our sins in his body on the tree [Calvary]" (1 Peter 2:24 RSV). Whether you immediately experience a sense of forgiveness or not, you can rest on the sheer promise of God that your sins have been "blotted out." It is a matter of accepting the integrity of God's Word. The inward sense of forgiveness may follow later. Do not confuse the *fact* of what Christ has done with your own feelings. Normally our *feelings,* which vary with individuals, follow.

There are many references in the Bible to forgiveness but let us cite two pertinent verses: Ephesians 1:7: "In whom we have redemption through his blood, the forgiveness of sins," and Ephesians 4:32: " . . . even as God for Christ's sake hath forgiven you."

2. *New life in Christ.* Despite the teaching of the church to the contrary, the idea persists that becoming a Christian involves a reformation process. We vaguely feel we are

turning over a new leaf or taking a step like making a New Year's resolution. Yet our best intentions seem always to fail.

This is not the case when you become a Christian. Something far more radical occurs. You become a new being (creation) in Christ. Externally you continue to be the same person. The new life results from an unseen spiritual transaction. By faith we must accept God's Word that it takes place. Both you and those around you will be aware of the change as time proceeds. Haven't you heard people say, "He's a changed person"?

Such a person eats the same food, wears the same clothing, sleeps in the same bed, but there is a discernible new quality about him that is known to all his associates. That is because he has experienced a *new* birth, possesses a *new* heart, a *new* nature. He is a new creation!

3. *The Holy Spirit comes to indwell you.* Perhaps the most astounding development of all for the new Christian is the fact that God in the person of the Holy Spirit comes to live in the believer's heart. Again this great fact may not be visible but it is very real. The Holy Spirit sent by God "into our heart" makes our bodies his "temple." In fact, "any one who does not have the Spirit of Christ [the Holy Spirit] does not belong to him" (Romans 8:9 RSV).

If the new believer allows the Holy Spirit to control his being, the heavenly guest will produce his "fruit" in our lives: "love, joy, peace, patience, kindness, goodness, faithfulness, gentleness, self-control" (Galatians 5:22, 23 RSV).

4. *You become a member of Christ's body, the church.* Up to this juncture, the stress has been upon the new Christian's individual experiences. As D. Reginald Thomas, eloquent Welsh-born preacher, has pointed out, new life in Christ closely resembles our physical birth. Being born is a personal, individual experience. But the moment we are born we become a part of a family. So it is in the spiritual realm. The new birth is personal, but once we are alive in

Christ we happily discover that we have been born into the family of God, the church. We are no longer alone. Henceforth the one-time alien is an integral part of the community of the redeemed.

So closely are we related to other Christians that the Bible, in explaining the relationship, uses the analogy of the human body: "For by one Spirit are we all baptized into one body" (1 Corinthians 12:13). There is an organic, not an organizational, relationship of Christians. By baptism we openly declare this relationship with the particular, local, and visible church. While it is true that we have been born into the world-wide communion of all believers, it is in the local manifestation of the universal church that one has the experience of fellowship, worship, and service.

Malcolm Muggeridge, the noted British writer and editor, graphically recounts his own dramatic experience of confrontation with Jesus Christ:

> This is how I came to see my situation, in a sort of dream or vision; something more vivid and actual than most happenings and experiences. I am confined in the tiny dark dungeon of my ego; manacled with the appetites of the flesh, shackled with the inordinate demands of the will—a prisoner serving a life sentence with no hope of deliverance. Then I notice that high above me there is a window through which a faint glow of light comes filtering in. Seemingly so far away, so remote and inaccessible; yet I realize a window looking out onto eternity. Inside darkness, a place of fantasies and furies; outside, the white radiance of God's love shining through the universe, what the Apostle Paul called the glorious liberty of the children of God.
>
> And the window? I know what that is too—the Incarnation. Time and eternity intersecting in a cross; now becoming Always. God revealing Himself as a man, and reaching down to us, in order that we, reaching up, may relate ourselves to Him. Now I observe that the window is not, after all, far away, but near at hand, and that seen through it everything makes sense; as it were, comes into sync, so that like the blind man whose sight Jesus restored, I can say: "One thing I know, that whereas I was blind,

now I see. Thenceforth, whenever I am looking through the window I see life as being full of joy and hope and brotherliness. . . ."[3]

There are many in our secular society who explain Christian conversion in terms of psychological experience. They seek to explain the phenomenon as an emotional condition triggered by some trauma. This results in a type of personality change, they say. Some experts might add that some people are more psychically susceptible to such "conversions," much as one might be to hypnosis or certain drugs.

But to explain new life in Christ in such terms completely misses what spiritual regeneration means. The new birth results because God has done something in the depths of our being. Those who have been "dead" to God and his Christ are now "alive" in the truest sense. Love for both God and neighbor mark the full response of the new man in Christ.

It is impossible in this short book to describe all that takes place when one becomes a Christian. But again we stress that new *life* in Christ is essential before one can experience *growth*. It should also be declared that virtually all the dynamics of the new birth are at work in the new life as growth takes place: Jesus Christ, the work of the Holy Spirit, the Holy Scriptures, and church fellowship.

All of these are important. Indeed these are all indispensable and work simultaneously for our benefit. Yet if we want to experience joyful, fruitful life it is important that we comprehend the basic importance of our *union with Jesus Christ*. Too often works dealing with spiritual growth do not give adequate attention to this unique aspect of the new life. We must not make that mistake here.

3. Malcolm Muggeridge, Message given at International Conference on Evangelism, Lausanne, 1974.

3

It Starts with a Shared Life

When Grace Kelly, a movie actress from Philadelphia, was married to Prince Rainier III of Monaco, there was a great change in her style of life. A commoner became a princess.

Even more dramatic are the implications for the forgiven sinner who is united to Jesus Christ. This is the fundamental aspect of Christianity. Union with Christ is the unique and essential relationship that provides the potential for Christian growth.

This union with Christ does not mean we lose our identity as persons. Actually, our organic spiritual identification with Jesus Christ enhances our own personality and liberates us from the bondage of our old life of self-centeredness. Despite the many distorted representations by those within and outside the household of faith, the Christian life is a joyous adventure.

There are many paradoxes within the Christian faith. For example, the Apostle Paul speaks about being a bondslave of Jesus Christ, and that is a proper analogy. Yet the believer who is willing to submit himself discovers that this is the surest way to discover freedom and fulfilment.

Our great example in the freedom-through-bondage role is the Lord Jesus himself: "'Among you, whoever wants to be great must be your servant, and whoever wants to be first must be willing slave of all—like the Son of Man; he did not come to be served, but to serve, and to give up his life as a ransom for many'" (Matthew 20:26–28 NEB).

The principles of the Kingdom of God are quite unlike those that operate in the secular world. It is necessary to pursue a radically different approach if we are to make any progress as Christians.

Submitting to the divine principles of successful living means recognizing from the outset that we must observe the ground rules of the one who has become our master. The oldest creed of the Christian faith, first uttered by the believers of the infant church, is "Jesus Christ is Lord." That means that we acknowledge the authority of Christ's lordship over our entire life. We do this, not as robots, but willingly.

At first this fills our heart with fear. It is a threat to our egocentric character. It would appear that our very being is going to be overwhelmed.

C. S. Lewis describes his reluctant entrance into new life: "In the Trinity Term of 1929 I gave in, and admitted that God was God, and knelt and prayed: perhaps, that night the most dejected and reluctant convert in all England . . . But who can duly adore the Love which will open high the gates to a prodigal who is brought in kicking, struggling, resentful, and darting his eyes in every direction for a chance of escape? . . . The hardness of God is kinder than the softness of men, and His compulsion is our liberation."[1]

There is no denying that it is hard for us to accept the concept that we have a new boss. He is Lord and he is King!

But here is the paradox: Once we submit to this lordship

---

1. C. S. Lewis, *Surprised by Joy*, New York: Harcourt, Brace & Co., 1956.

we find that in that very act of subjugation we come "into the glorious liberty of the children of God" (Romans 8:21). All of the guidelines of our individualistic culture exalt the concept of the "self-made man." What a travesty that countless people accept this false gospel of worldly attainment.

St. Augustine describes his own struggles in submitting to the lordship of Christ, "hugging the fleeting world . . ." and "yet was I drawing nearer by little and little, and unconsciously."[2]

Yet the very Lord who demands our submission to his authority empowers us to carry out his commands. Now we come back once more to what I believe is the basic truth of our Christian faith: our union with Jesus Christ.

St. Paul repeatedly uses the strange expression "in Christ." We have already encountered the phrase in the passage, "If any one is in Christ, he is a new creation" (2 Corinthians 5:17 RSV). In another key sentence Paul says, "For as in Adam all die, so also in Christ shall all be made alive" (1 Corinthians 15:22 RSV). Even more astounding is the revelation that we were chosen "in him before the foundation of the world" (Ephesians 1:4).

Nothing perplexes us more than the idea that God chooses us. The idea that this choice was made "in Christ" before the foundation of the world sounds fatalistic. Since God is eternal and sovereign, he is not bound by the time-space limitations of our world. We try in vain to fit God and his actions into our human logic. It is best to accept his initiating, loving grace and rest in his loving concern for us.

Let us move along to another baffling concept. How can one person be *in* another person in the way St. Paul uses the expression?

Is this semantic nonsense or, as Scripture seems to indi-

2. St. Augustine, *Confessions*, Everyman's Library, E. P. Dutton & Co., Inc., 1907.

cate, one of the most significant facts of human existence?

Being "in Christ" relates to what Christ accomplished at Calvary when he overcame Satan and his domain and created a new order. "The phrase 'in Christ' is an epigram for the total reality of the new community under Christ's lordship, a community called by His voice, ruled by His Spirit, and forming the embryo of a total new race and a whole new creation united and renewed by Him."[3]

Here is the bedrock truth which makes it possible for you to become a growing (maturing) Christian. The dynamic of our ongoing life stems from our organic relationship to Christ himself. He explains this in the analogy of the vine: "I am the vine, ye are the branches: He that abideth in me, and I in him, the same bringeth forth much fruit: for without me ye can do nothing" (John 1:5).

Can you conceive of a bunch of grapes growing to maturity on a branch that has been broken off the grapevine? Just as preposterous is the concept that Christians can divorce themselves from their source of life (Jesus Christ) and lead an autonomous existence.

Yet how often one hears the comment, "I feel I could never live the Christian life." And that is true. None of us can take one step in the Christian life on our own; that is, in our own strength.

Even the talented and imposing figure of St. Paul realized his impotence apart from Christ. Hear him explain it: "I have been crucified with Christ; it is no longer I who live, but Christ who lives in me; and the life I now live in the flesh I live by faith in the Son of God, who loved me and gave himself for me" (Galatians 2:20 RSV).

I know this verse may present as many problems as it may solve. What, for instance, does Paul mean by the statement that he has been crucified with Christ? Is this some sub-

3. Lewis B. Smedes, *All Things Made New*, Grand Rapids: Eerdmans, 1970.

jective and mystical experience that ordinary human beings cannot comprehend? After all, Paul did not meet Christ on the Damacus road until long after the crucifixion. We know that at a certain point in time the Incarnate One died on the Cross for our sins. Paul seems to be saying that Christ died *for* us but that he (and we, too) died *with* him. The Apostle takes up the theme in depth in Romans 6: "Do you not know that all of us who have been baptized into Christ Jesus were baptized into his death?" (Romans 6:3 RSV).

Before we get mired down we must understand each step of Paul's logic. The readers of his original letter to the Romans would have understood his references to baptism. They knew that baptism followed immediately upon confession of faith in Christ. The rite of baptism marked the end of the old life, the beginning of the new. To be baptized was to be "buried." This rite was the formal declaration by the new believer that his old life, or old way of life, had ended. He was "buried" with Christ.

So Paul continues: "We were buried therefore with him by baptism into death, so that as Christ was raised from the dead by the glory of the Father, we too might walk in newness of life" (Romans 6:4 RSV).

Thus, Christ not only died *for* us. We died representatively *with* him, and rose again from the dead with him. Just how far do we carry the analogy of death and resurrection? We are faced with the fact that Christ died on the Cross nearly 2,000 years ago and most Christians who read this were born in the twentieth century.

Roman Catholics and those in the Catholic tradition hold that the baptismal rite is the causal instrument in being joined to Christ. Protestants insist that baptism has meaning only in the context of faith.

But baptism is more than a *subjective* experience. A modern Jew in observing the Passover might say, "We were slaves to the Pharaoh in Egypt and the Lord our God brought *us* forth." Obviously the modern Jew is identifying himself with the community which was redeemed at the Exodus. He is a part of that continuing community.

"To be baptized into the death of Christ, and so to die and be raised with Him, is to share the life of the community that was created by the redemptive acts of the Cross and the resurrection."[4]

But there is more, as Paul explains in the crucial sixth chapter of Romans. Baptism marks the individual believer's identification with the Lord Jesus Christ and his people (the church). "The man we once were has been crucified with Christ" (Romans 6:6 NEB). This "crucifixion" is not a present experience but a past event. Those who are united to Christ by faith are considered by God as having been crucified with Christ.

If in the mind of God our identification with Christ is spiritually true, it can become practically and presently true if we *reckon* ourselves to be "dead to sin but alive unto God."

Perhaps we can better understand this basic aspect of the means of becoming a growing Christian if we refer back to a portion of Scripture discussed earlier.

"He [God] hath chosen us in him [Christ] before the foundation of the world, that we should be holy and without blame before him in love" (Ephesians 1:4).

Since we were not present before the world was formed, it would appear that this is a truth we must accept by faith. Likewise "reckoning" ourselves dead to sin and alive to God is more than a mental exercise. It is a profound and spiritually effective means of walking by faith and experiencing, with the Holy Spirit's aid, a glorious procession of new adventures in Christ's company.

I must admit that for many years I dodged the truth of our dying with Christ. The people who talked about this

4. Lewis B. Smedes, *All Things Made New*, Grand Rapids: Eerdmans, 1970.

kind of identification with Christ seemed to be demanding a special step of faith I did not want to take. The whole concept of crucifixion with Christ suggested a lugubrious sort of existence. To be honest, it repelled me.

But I realize now that this is not an option open only to a spiritual minority. That we have died with Christ is true of every Christian, no matter how ignorant he may be of its implications. It is a basic truth that applies to every believer. It is not true that only a special class of believers has come into higher truth. It is not that some Christians have "experienced crucifixion" and others have not.

Our identification with Jesus Christ—our union with him—is an objective fact. The practical reality of the fact comes home to us when we reckon it to be true by faith.

St. Paul expresses it clearly: "Always bearing about in the body the dying of the Lord Jesus, that the life also of Jesus might be made manifest in our body" (2 Corinthians 4:10).

What is God's purpose in redeeming us? To take us to heaven? To save us from hell? To make us good? Yes, but his ultimate goal for his redeemed children is that they "be conformed to the image of his Son" (Romans 8:29; see also 1 John 3:2). In other words, by a long process, not an overnight one, God is seeking to conform us morally, spiritually, totally so that we will take on the likeness of Jesus Christ.

The process of changing us (called sanctification) starts with our new birth and is only completed when we come into the presence of the Lord. Bearing the image of Christ seems so unattainable. How many Christians do you know that remind you of Jesus Christ?

Since I have been involved in Christian work most of my adult life, my wife and I are acquainted with a large sampling of believers representing every segment of Christendom. One day, as we were talking together, one of us asked the other: "Who among our friends reminds you most of Jesus Christ?"

Both of us pondered that one a long time. We had known a number of prominent leaders in all circles—the very orthodox, the ecumenical, the activistic, the literate and articulate.

"But who," we persisted, "most bears a resemblance to Christ?"

We could list the excellent attributes of many. But likeness to Christ? That was something else. It disturbed us deeply to realize how few there were who had genuinely Christ-like qualities.

We finally mentioned the names of two women, wives of good men who had devoted their lives to Christ's service. Out of the hundreds of people we knew, we came up with only two candidates. What a commentary!

Growth in grace and the knowledge of Jesus Christ is another way of describing the process of being conformed to Christ's image. God first made man in his own "image" and "likeness" and seemingly was thwarted by the entrance of sin into his perfect creation. But God will not be prevented from attaining his ultimate purpose. Through his reconciling work, Christ, who is "the express image" of God, provides the means by which the divine purpose will be achieved. The people of God will all bear the image of God when redemptive history is consummated.

You may say that this is all very wonderful but it seems so remote. It is an eternity away. What about my day-by-day growth here and now? And that is a fair question.

The thrust of this chapter is that in the redemptive program of God all Christians are intimately and organically related to Jesus Christ himself. In the language of the King James Version we are "partakers of the divine nature." The New English Bible translates it even more vividly: We have "come to share in the very being of God" (2 Peter 1:4).

We are not left to cope alone with the challenges and problems of life and the contradictions of our own personalities. Our Lord's parting promise to his disciples was

"I am with you always," but it goes beyond his presence *with* us. The surging resurrection life of Christus Victor is *in* each believer. It is because of this inner shared life that "we all reflect as in a mirror the splendour of the Lord; thus we are transfigured into his likeness from splendour to splendour . . ." (2 Corinthians 3:18 NEB).

The obvious teaching of Scripture is that those who are vitally linked with Christ will demonstrate Christ-like qualities, and that becomes a progressive movement in our lives from "one glory to another."

Most of us have to confess that we are not aware of much growth. We are more conscious of the secret surges of selfishness and pride, the hot anger or smouldering jealousy, and the unholy desire for position and place.

Do you not realize that God knows your heart? He knows "our frame," the Psalmist declares. Provision has been made for solving this dilemma that plagues every believer: "If we confess our sins, he is faithful and just to forgive us our sins, and to cleanse us from all unrighteousness" (1 John 1:9).

The Bible does not teach perfectionism. We do not become little tin gods. But the marvelous fact of redemption is that we are forever joined to the source of life. Even though we start out as "babes in Christ," by God's grace we have the capacity for growth.

In addition to our union with Christ, there are other "means of grace" which help us in our push toward spiritual maturity. They work concurrently and harmoniously with this fundamental fact of our life in Christ. We shall see that the quiet, selfless, internal ministry of the Holy Spirit, that the instrumentality of Word and sacrament, and that the fellowship in the Body of Christ are parts of a holy mosaic. We cannot dispense with any of these divinely decreed provisions for our growth in grace and the knowledge of our Lord and Savior Jesus Christ.

4

Tenant with a Lifetime Lease

I have made several trips to Asia, and I have met a number of Buddhists. We have talked about Buddhism on a number of occasions but never once have I heard a Buddhist say that the great Siddhartha Gautama was somehow living inside him. My Asian friends would be polite in true Oriental fashion but they would think I was insane if I were to ask if the Buddha was in any sense personally present within them.

But Christianity teaches just such an astounding truth— that God in the person of his Holy Spirit indwells every believer. God's Spirit makes his home within us. No other world religion makes such a fantastic claim.

One hears much more about the Holy Spirit and his ministry nowadays than formerly. There was a time when not much was said about the Holy Spirit except perhaps in certain holiness and Pentecostal circles. To much of the church the third person of the Trinity was, as someone described him, "the Half Known God."

While the holiness and other related groups were accused of emphasizing subjective Christian experience, Reformed theology and Fundamentalism stressed the importance of the Bible in Christian growth. Theoretically, they held a doctrine of the Holy Spirit, but no one did very much about it. They looked askance at those whom they felt came down too strongly on experience rather than the objective truth of Scripture.

But the Holy Spirit is God and shares an equal place with the Father and Son in the Holy Trinity. And the Scriptures have a good deal to say about the Spirit's activity in bringing us to maturity.

Nevertheless, considerable controversy clouds the means by which the Spirit's power is appropriated. The phenomenal growth of the Pentecostal movement has forced all concerned Christians to re-examine such doctrines as "the baptism in the Holy Spirit" and "the gifts of the Spirit." All in the church should be humble enough to admit that we owe much to the Pentecostals for making the Holy Spirit a topic of conversation. Furthermore, only the most partisan Christian would dismiss the vitality of the charismatic movement whether it be in the historic Pentecostal denominations, in the major Protestant communions, or in the Roman Catholic Church.

But feelings against the charismatic renewal, as the neo-Pentecostal movement is called, are so strong that there are many who would write it off completely as the work of Satan.

Because of its non-theological emphasis, the new Pentecostalism does present some challenges to a church that has given little place to the person and work of the Holy Spirit.

Let us step back and try to discover what the Bible has to say and seek to avoid the acrimony of the current debate. A knowledge of how the Holy Spirit works is essential to any treatment of Christian growth. Indeed, there is no growth apart from the work of the Holy Spirit.

John R. W. Stott, noted Anglican evangelical, says, "The

fullness of the Holy Spirit is one of the distinctive blessings of the new age."[1] Since the Holy Spirit is God, he is eternal. He was involved in creation, providence, revelation, and equipping chosen people for certain tasks in the history of Israel. We possess the Scriptures because the Spirit inspired "holy men of old."

John the Baptist told the world of his day that God's Messiah would make the Holy Spirit available to all: "I have baptized you with water," says the Baptist, "but he [Christ] will baptize you with the Holy Spirit" (Mark 1:8 RSV). It is Christ who would inaugurate the new era in human history and Christ himself would be "the baptizer." At our regeneration we are the beneficiaries of a "package deal": (1) our sins are put away and (2) we receive a baptizing with the Holy Spirit. Thus every believer becomes the recipient of the Holy Spirit, whether he is recognized or not.

The exaltation of Jesus Christ to the throne of heaven was antecedent to his "pouring out" the Holy Spirit at Pentecost, a milestone in redemptive history. The Apostle Peter on the day of Pentecost cried: "Repent, and be baptized every one of you in the name of Jesus Christ for the forgiveness of your sins; and you shall receive the gift of the Holy Spirit" (Acts 2:38 RSV).

Stott points out that we must never conceive of salvation as the negative putting away of sins only. We must always include the positive blessings of the indwelling Holy Spirit.

Water baptism is the outer symbol of initiation into Christ. The Spirit baptism is the inner reality. It is at this juncture that the individual believer is joined to the larger company, the Body of Christ. "For by one Spirit are we all baptized into one body . . . and have been all made to

1. John R. W. Stott, *The Baptism and Fullness of the Holy Spirit*, Downers Grove, Ill.: Inter-Varsity Press, 1964.

drink into one Spirit. For the body is not one member, but many" (1 Corinthians 12:13, 14).

The descent of the Holy Spirit at Pentecost was a historic event, a dramatic occurrence that resulted in the believers being filled with the Spirit, and speaking in foreign languages (not previously known to them) and making prophetic utterances. This supernatural endowment of the ability to speak other languages forms the crux of the difference between the teaching of Pentecostals and other Christians. Essentially Pentecostals and charismatics teach that the phenomena of Pentecost are not only related to a historic event but also serve as the pattern for the normative experience of every seeking believer. Thus the baptism in the Holy Spirit (an inner work) is accompanied by the external evidence—the believer speaking in a tongue, either a known foreign language or what is sometimes called an "unknown tongue" or "a heavenly language." Pentecostals base their belief on a number of Scripture passages, but the most important are those describing believers being baptized in the Spirit and speaking in tongues after Pentecost. (See Acts 10:45, 46; 8:17; 11:15-17; 19:6.)

Pentecostals generally teach that baptism in the Holy Spirit is an experience subsequent to conversion (regeneration) and is marked by tongues speaking. The rest of the evangelical world as well as other sections of the church teach only that all believers are indwelt by the Holy Spirit and that his presence (initially or in subsequent experience) is not necessarily attended by tongues speaking.

But all Christians, including Pentecostals, have much more in common than this single difference of interpretation would indicate. Furthermore, the late R. A. Torrey as well as other respected non-Pentecostal evangelicals described the baptism in the Holy Spirit as an exhilarating and energizing experience that comes after conversion.

It is somewhat embarrassing to admit that there is so

much controversy in the church over the vital doctrine of the Holy Spirit's empowerment of believers. There are other groups that oppose tongues speaking but strongly press for being filled with the Spirit—an experience that is subsequent to conversion. Many British and American evangelicals advocate this doctrine.

What has come to be known in the United States particularly as the "victorious life" teaching probably received its original impetus nearly a century ago at the Keswick Convention in England's Lake Country. Since then "Keswicks" have sprung up in various parts of the world, popularized by itinerant Bible teachers and writers.

The "victorious life" which results from the conscious experience of being filled with the Spirit can become a reality for any believer. The seeker must first ask forgiveness of any known sin in his life, recognizing his own spiritual emptiness, and then by faith accept the fulness of the Spirit. This experience of being filled by the Spirit is not regarded as a once-for-all event but may be followed by other fillings to meet the believer's need for spiritual strengthening. Most of the proponents of Keswick truth would speak of "one baptism, many fillings." The emphasis is upon God's willingness to fill us as we are willing to be recipients by faith alone, without the baptism in the Spirit as a subsequent experience, or attended by tongues speaking.

Both Pentecostals who advocate baptism in the Spirit as a subsequent experience to conversion and the "victorious life" school which advocates the fulness of the Spirit are essentially seeking the same goal for the believer: the means for growth in Christ and for more effective Christian service. Both groups are correct in assessing the need for divine energizing and in realizing that the work of the Lord cannot be accomplished by human effort.

The individuals in the New Testament who are described as being filled with the Spirit, including John the Baptist, his mother Elizabeth, his father Zachariah, Peter, Paul, and others in the apostolic company, seem in every instance to have possessed spiritual power for a specific prophetic utterance or mission. The emphasis in the text is on the particular event in each case.

But when others, such as our Lord himself, Stephen, and Barnabas, were said to be "full of the Holy Spirit," this probably describes an abiding state of fulness of the Holy Spirit. Stephen, for example, *was full of the Spirit because his life was marked by a consistent obedient response to God's love and grace.* He submitted to the lordship of Christ and obeyed from the heart. Thus the indwelling Holy Spirit was the dominant and habitual influence in his life. The Holy Spirit did not fill him by formula or by crisis experience.

There is actually only a single statement in the New Testament that Christians are to be filled with the Spirit: "And be not drunk with wine, wherein is excess; but be filled with the Spirit" (Ephesians 5:18). There is no denying the use here of the imperative mood. The Ephesians passage appears to emphasize the contrast between the profligate man who becomes "soaked" with wine (that is the thrust of the word "drunk") as opposed to the believer filled with the Holy Spirit. In both cases the individual is "under the influence" of a prevailing power.

The analogy of being filled with the Holy Spirit should not be thought of as a liquid being poured into a vessel. Rather the indwelling Holy Spirit is the dominating influence of the believer's life. Being filled with the Spirit has such influence when the believer has been obedient to the commandments of his Lord.

It should also be noted that in the Ephesians passage the injunction to be filled with the Spirit is followed by the suggestion that Christians minister, or communicate with one another by singing "psalms and hymns and spiritual songs." The context of this biblical text, at least, does not seem to support the idea that being filled with the Spirit results in strengthening for service. Rather it is related to worship and fellowship.

Should we be embarrassed by these differences of interpretation? I think not. Most of the epistles of the New Testament were written to deal with problems, wrong emphases in the Christian faith, and moral issues arising out of a failure to give heed to "sound teaching." Out of the crucible of the difficulties of the churches of apostolic times we have received the New Testament.

Teaching about the Holy Spirit is vital for every Christian who wants to grow. Let us follow the example of the ancient Bereans who "received the word with all readiness of mind and searched the scriptures daily, whether those things were so" (Acts 17:11). In other words, let each believer be settled in his own mind about the great teachings of our faith. With our minds and hearts illuminated by the Holy Spirit, we must turn to the Scriptures ourselves. Whether it is a crisis experience or the Spirit's abiding presence in our lives, St. Paul indicates that the possession of the Holy Spirit is the distinguishing mark of a Christian.

"But ye are not in the flesh, but in the Spirit, if so be that the Spirit of God dwell in you. Now if any man have not the Spirit of Christ, he is none of his" (Romans 8:9).

It is important that we notice that in this passage the Holy Spirit is called "the Spirit of Christ," and so he is. The indwelling of the Holy Spirit and the indwelling of Christ are referred to interchangeably. Christ dwells or abides in the believer by his Spirit. He (the Spirit) is the functioning Christ. "The Holy Spirit is the living contact between the victorious Lord and Savior and all who are united with Him."[2]

2. Lewis B. Smedes, *All Things Made New*, Grand Rapids: Eerdmans, 1970.

While our Lord was still with his disciples he told them that the Holy Spirit would come as "the comforter."

(The word "comforter," used in the King James Version, means "one who is called to someone's aid" or "one who appears in another's behalf." Various translations employ different synonyms such as "counselor," "advocate," "helper," etc. This is the function of the Holy Spirit. Like Christ himself, the Spirit, though fully God, takes on a servant role, never exalting himself, but always glorifying Jesus Christ.)

Further, the Lord Jesus declared that the Holy Spirit would guide the disciples "into all truth." Indeed he is called "the Spirit of Truth." Here we touch upon a primary function of the Spirit—providing us with guidance to do what is right. Of this we will have more to say later.

After instructing the Galatians about the freedom in Christ to serve one another in love, the Apostle Paul warns that if they bite and devour one another, they will be consumed.

". . . I say then, Walk in the Spirit, and ye shall not fulfil the lust of the flesh" (Galatians 5:16).

Then the Apostle lists the various "works of the flesh" and warns that "they which do such things shall not inherit the kingdom of God" (Galatians 5:21).

In contrast, Paul next describes the "fruit of the Spirit"— the analogy that gives us the best picture of what Christian character really is. Our Lord Jesus who was always full of the Spirit exhibited all of these graces in his life. No doubt, Paul had this in mind when he declared, "For me to live is Christ" (Philippians 1.21).

If you want to know what is meant by Christian character and how we may measure our growth in Christ, study Galatians 5:22, 23. Here we discover the nine-fold cluster of Christian graces: love, joy, peace, patience, kindness, goodness, faithfulness, gentleness, and self-control. (Please note the use of the singular "fruit" rather than "fruits," suggesting the unity and harmony of the Spirit's work.)

The fruit of the Holy Spirit is not to be confused with the gifts of the Holy Spirit. These beautiful aspects of Christian character (the fruit) are available to *every* believer. The gifts or charisms of the Spirit, such as those of faith or healing, are sovereignly distributed to believers *as the Spirit wills.* Such gifts do not affect Christian character. They are specialized endowments given to certain believers for the upbuilding of the Body of Christ. Their place will be discussed in the chapter on the church.

This cluster of nine graces can never be produced by the "flesh," or unregenerate human nature, although volumes have been written about them in all genres of literature. The erroneous concept persists in secular literature that man is essentially good and that these qualities can erupt and grow in any one of us. But this is the deception of deceptions. The Bible teaches that only the new man in Christ is possessed of the Holy Spirit, and only the Holy Spirit can produce the fruit of Christian character. "This is produced *in* the believer not *by* the believer."[3]

This is not to deny that non-Christians often demonstrate a quality of life that exceeds that of many professing Christians. How do we explain this contradiction?

Human beings, created originally in the "image and likeness" of God, still possess capacities that are unknown to other living creatures. May we borrow a term from the evolutionists and describe these admirable qualities as "vestigial remains" of our earlier estate? Some Reformed theologians describe this capacity of unregenerate men to perform good works as "common grace," which it is argued, restrains the destructive process of inherent sin.

More recently a new breed of secular sociobiologists has

3. Lewis Sperry Chafer, *He That Is Spiritual,* Grand Rapids: Zondervan, 1918.

surfaced which dubs altruism as "genetic selfishness."[4] This smacks of a new type of determinism that ultimately demeans our humanity and robs man of sentience and responsibility.

There are aspects of human behavior that are described in our parlance as "love" which cannot be equated with the self-giving active response of Christian love. Our culture is permeated with the idea that the ultimate in human experience is the ecstatic, absorbing emotion of physical love. Our creator God is responsible for our sexuality and if his ground rules are followed, erotic love has an essential place in our well-being. But the line between legitimate and illegitimate affection is often transgressed. We must not equate physical infatuation with responsible affection, even at the human level. How easily passionate infatuation turns to violent hatred. But real love is always kind and self-effacing.

It is almost impossible to cut through the semantic jungle to get at the facts. Man's most sordid behavior—adultery, fornication, uncleanness and lasciviousness—is often referred to as "love" in the shoddy mixed-up world where most of us live. In contrast, C. S. Lewis has written sensitively on the four Greek words rendered as "love" in English. He points out that there are legitimate aspects of the "natural" loves but divine love not only supersedes, but enriches, them.[5]

We are dealing with *agape* love when we discuss the fruit of the Spirit. This is divine, self-giving love. In what other strength can one ever *love* one's enemies? It is significant that when St. Paul enjoins husbands to love their wives, he employs the word for agape love. Does this not indicate that

4. Edward O. Wilson, *Sociobiology: The New Synthesis*, Cambridge, Mass.: Harvard University Press, 1977.

5. C. S. Lewis, *The Four Loves*, New York: Harcourt, Brace and Company, 1960.

our limited natural love, no matter how romantic, cannot energize a strong enough concern for the stresses that come into any marriage relationship? If we are seeking to grow in moral stature, we must experience this primary fruit of the Spirit. How does this love enter our being? The Apostle Paul gives the answer: "The love of God is shed abroad in our hearts by the Holy Ghost which is given unto us." The NEB phrases it: "God's love has flooded our inmost heart through the Holy Spirit . . ." (Romans 5:5).

Our behavior will be immature, no matter how old we are, or how long we have been Christians, if we do not know something about this "imparted love."

The second spiritual quality of the nine-fold cluster is joy. There is nothing more impressive than a person who genuinely exudes joy. Listening to the conversation of people one hears the constant refrain of criticism of others or griping about circumstances. All of us have been guilty of this immature conduct. We nurse our grievances, real or imagined, and more often than not our faces betray our inner frustration and anger.

When a person possessed of genuine joy enters a room, it seems to change the emotional atmosphere. There is a contagious quality about joy. Joy, unlike happiness, is not dependent on external circumstances. Joy wells up from inside us. We cannot work it up by our own effort; it is generated within us by the indwelling Holy Spirit. It is closely associated with agape love.

How many cranky, long-faced Christians I have known! Some seem to equate a mournful expression with spirituality. Tightly entangled in a legalistic code as a rule of life, these poor souls seem to think it is sinful to laugh or to enjoy the common mercies that God so bountifully provides for us.

How twisted is the idea that proper doctrine mixed with a doleful expression can influence anyone for Christ. This is like the bondage Paul deals with in the Epistle to the Galatians. Fortunately, in this same segment of Scripture he also describes the freedom of "walking" in the Spirit and thereby inhibiting the desires of our lower nature.

In earlier years I knew a Scottish Bible teacher and pastor named James McGinlay. He was a bantam model of sartorial perfection and he always smelled good because he used perfume. (This was long before Brut was discovered.) He confided to me once that he used perfume "to the glory of God" because he didn't want to be offensive to "poor, dear souls" whom he might be counseling after descending in perspiration-soaked clothing from the pulpit.

On one occasion, McGinlay recounted, he visited a Christian book room in Toronto. Presiding over the establishment was a stern and righteous elderly woman, who took in my Scottish friend with a withering glance.

Holding her nose high in sniffing posture, she declared, "You use perfume!"

McGinlay batted not an eye; instead he sniffed back at her, saying, "You don't."

Maybe this is a farfetched illustration. After all, joy is not doused on us like perfume. But the evidence of joy in a Christian is pleasant incense to God and man.

Christian joy is not the synthetic "life of the party" quality. Indeed joy may paradoxically accompany suffering and sorrow for Christ's sake: "As sorrowful, yet always rejoicing" (2 Corinthians 6:10).

Let us survey briefly each of the other fruit of the Spirit.

"Peace," which is basically the same as the Old Testament word, "shalom," means "completeness," "soundness," "well-being." It conveys much more than the negative idea of the absence of conflict. Peace is a supernatural serenity that issues only from the indwelling Holy Spirit.

"Longsuffering" in the KJV ("patience" in the RSV and NEB) suggests a kind of tolerance that suffers fools, if not gladly, at least patiently. Perhaps "forbearance" is another way of saying it. "Kindness" suggests "goodness" and "generosity." "Goodness" is self-evident. "Faith" probably should be more exactly rendered as "reliability" or "faithfulness." "Meekness" could also be translated "humility." "Temperance" is better rendered "self-control," yet the "control" emanates not from "self" but from the Holy Spirit who enables the new man in Christ to be "moderate" or "temperate."

Thus the fruit of the Spirit when carefully considered is a veritable harvest of Christian virtue. These are the Christlike qualities that demonstrate spiritual maturity. But these graces do not appear automatically. There must be a conscious effort on the believer's part "to walk in the Spirit," that is, to walk by means of the Spirit. There is no more important principle of Christian growth.

Perhaps two more things should be said about the Christian's attitude toward the indwelling Holy Spirit. Both are presented negatively in Scripture:

"Quench not the Spirit" (1 Thessalonians 5:19) and "grieve not the Spirit" (Ephesians 4:30).

It is only possible to "quench" a light or a fire. The Spirit who brings warmth and light to the Christian life should be allowed to have free course. There are always proper Christians who fear that any sort of enthusiasm is disruptive or in bad taste. If the Apostle Paul sought to curb excessive zeal in the Corinthian church, he must have given the opposite advice to the Thessalonians. Some of them may have been despondent because Christ had not returned for them, as they had expected from Paul's earlier preaching.

Only *persons* can be "grieved," which underscores the fact that the Holy Spirit is a person. The injunction not to grieve him is set in a context dealing with misuse of the tongue. "No bad language must pass your lips, but only what is good and helpful to the occasion . . . Have done with spite and passion, all angry shouting and cursing, and bad feeling of every kind" (Ephesians 4:29, 31 NEB).

Conduct unbecoming a Christian "grieves" the Holy Spirit, whose presence is the seal of our inheritance in Christ.

There is no better place than this to assert that our union with Christ cannot be separated from the work of the Holy Spirit in bringing us to Christian maturity. For us maturity means a growing likeness to our Lord and Savior who is also our Exemplar. No life more completely exhibits the graces listed as the fruit of the Spirit than our Lord's. As we permit the Holy Spirit to operate in our lives, the fruit will be evident in our character. That is another way of saying that we are growing in the likeness of Jesus Christ.

Likewise this process of growth is related to our place within the corporate community, the Body of Christ. In more than one place in Scripture it is recorded that the operating sphere of the Spirit is "the temple of God" (1 Corinthians 3:16, 17; 2 Corinthians 6:16). Here the temple of God is "the people of God," even though in 1 Corinthians 6:19 the same analogy of the temple refers to the bodies of individual believers. Thus there is an emphasis both on individual responsibility and on our life together in referring to the habitation of Holy Spirit. In our individualistic culture, the significance of our corporate existence is too often ignored. Christ and his Spirit can never be separated from the church which is his body. Any concept of growth which ignores this harmonious relationship of the various means of grace is foreign to divine revelation.

It is also impossible to assess the ministry of the Holy Spirit without concurrently discussing the role that the Word of God, or Holy Scripture, plays in our growth. Neither Holy Spirit nor Holy Scripture works independently. Both operate instrumentally and concomitantly to bring us into conformity to Jesus Christ. They play essential but servant roles in this process just as our Lord himself was servant in accomplishing his divine mission on earth.

This must be kept in mind as we examine in more detail the important place of Scripture in our growth in Christ.

5

Not by Bread Alone

Some years ago the writer was privileged to visit what was then the Dutch-ruled portion of the island of New Guinea. Faithful workers of the Christian and Missionary Alliance had preached the gospel to the naked cannibal tribes and they responded in great numbers. Because families and clans came en masse, it was called a people's movement. At first the missionaries were apprehensive about the overwhelming response to the message of Christ. Accustomed to one-by-one conversions, they feared the new believers were acting without knowledge.

But there were many distinguishing marks of faith in the new believers that convinced the mission's leadership that this was a bonafide movement of the Holy Spirit. When the western Dani tribe turned to the Lord, they wanted to hear all about the "Jesus way." The missionaries became hoarse and physically fatigued by repeatedly giving the Christian message to rapt throngs of eager believers. The tribespeople had an insatiable hunger for the Word of God. At the same time there were other changes in their lives: they burned their fetishes, they renounced the continual round of tribal warfare, they stopped beating their wives, they began to sing simple hymns adapted to old drinking tunes, and they began to reach out across the mountains to tell others about their new discovery of Christ. But the intense hunger for the Word of God was one of the first signs of their nascent life.

Here were cannibals who had never heard of a Creator God or his Son Jesus Christ. But when they heard the gospel their lives were drastically changed and they began to love the Word of God although they had previously never seen nor heard of a Bible.

It soon became apparent that it was the Bible which was the major force in the lives of these naked tribespeople who so recently had devoted themselves to warfare and cannibalism.

In more sophisticated parts of the world new records in Bible sales are being set. There seems to be no end of new versions of Scripture, yet ironically many Christians are biblical illiterates. One of my friends describes himself as a Sunday School dropout to explain his lack of Bible knowledge.

In evangelical circles there is much profession of orthodoxy and much frenetic activity, but meditation on the law of God is a forgotten practice. No doubt this explains the deadness of so many churches and the vast number of retarded Christians.

It is ironic that this condition prevails in the very segment of the church which prides itself on a high view of Scripture. Our Lord accused the Pharisees of his day of having a distorted understanding of the role of Scripture: "You search the scriptures, because you think that in them you have eternal life; and it is they that bear witness to me; yet you refuse to come to me that you may have life" (John 5:39, 40 RSV).

In a sense we cannot have too high a view of Scripture yet we must recognize that primarily it is instrumental in bringing us to Christ. Indeed, we would have no knowledge of God or Jesus Christ or how we may share in the divinely initiated reconciliation apart from Holy Scripture. But Scripture is not an end in itself. We must come to Christ himself for life.

The Apostle Peter explains how important a part the Scriptures play in our growth:

"As newborn babes, desire the sincere milk of the word, that ye may grow thereby" (1 Peter 2:2).

Our faith is based on the objective revelation of God who acted in history on our behalf. Scripture is the dependable account of these redemptive acts and also the authoritative interpretation of their meaning for us. "But these are written," says St. John (20:31), "that ye might believe that Jesus is the Christ, the Son of God; and that believing ye might have life through his name."

Long before the advent of Jesus Christ, the Psalmist spoke about the effectiveness of Scripture as a cleansing agent in a life:

"How can a young man keep his way pure? By guarding it according to thy word" (Psalm 119:9 RSV).

In the same portion the Psalmist continues:

"I have laid up thy word in my heart, that I might not sin against thee" (119:11 RSV).

And then he exults:

"I will meditate on thy precepts, and fix my eyes on thy ways. I will delight in thy statutes; I will not forget thy word" (119:15, 16 RSV).

It is David also who can restore to us the forgotten art of meditation: "Blessed is the man . . . [whose] delight is in the law of the Lord, and on his law he meditates day and night" (Psalm 1:1-2 RSV).

Please note that David's concept of meditation is a far cry from the contemporary fad of "transcendental meditation," the contribution of Hinduism. TM does not center the mind on an objectively given revelation. The Bible indicates that we are sentient beings with the ability to reason and hearts that can be attuned to hear the voice of a loving, personal God. We do not become absorbed in an impersonal universal mind. Instead we have as both our Savior and Exemplar the Lord Jesus, who was touched with the feelings of our infirmities.

Even from within the ranks of Christendom has come the charge that those who give great place to the Bible's authority are guilty of bibliolatry. No doubt there is a danger of concentrating on the words of Holy Writ like the ancient Pharisees and not realizing that the Scriptures have as their great goal making Jesus Christ known to the heart and mind.

The Bible is not a paper pope, a Koran, or a sort of divine traffic code, giving us the do's and don'ts of proper conduct. True, the Bible does contain the Ten Commandments and the Sermon on the Mount. The Apostle Paul also tells us that the law is "holy, and just and good."

But because of the very perfection of holy law we become frustrated. The law sets a standard for us but it only serves to spotlight our sin and incompleteness. What utter arrogance is displayed by an individual who has the temerity to say that he lives by the Golden Rule or the Sermon on the Mount.

St. Paul says, "A man is not justified by works of the law but through faith in Jesus Christ. . . ." Contrarily he says "By the works of the law shall no one be justified" (Galatians 2:16 RSV). Again the Apostle says, "If justification were through the law, then Christ died to no purpose" (Galatians 2:21 RSV).

Just as we do not become Christians in the first place through "law keeping," neither can we as believers seek to lead an exemplary life through adherence to any code, even though it be handed down from heaven by Almighty God.

St. Paul argues that for believers to seek to live by keeping the law is like submitting themselves to "a yoke of slavery." It is in this context that the Apostle urges believers "to walk by the Spirit"—a wholly different way of conducting themselves. The wonderful secret of the new order initiated by Christ on the Cross is that his people may enjoy freedom and may live under the powerful dynamic force of the indwelling Holy Spirit.

We must erase from our minds the concept that we can grow by using the Bible as a rule book.

Nor is the Bible a talisman. During World War II, there were many stories of soldiers whose lives were saved by pocket Bibles. The enemy bullet was stopped when it struck the leaves of the Testament worn, say, in a soldier's breast pocket. A paperback novel could have accomplished the same protection. Nor is there magic in possessing a Bible. What a low view of the role of the Bible in bringing us to maturity.

John R. W. Stott says that supposing "that salvation lies in a book is as foolish as supposing that health lies in a prescription."[1] He continues with the analogy, showing how ridiculous it would be for the patient to take the prescription home to read it, study it, learn it by heart. The purpose of the prescription is to get us to the druggist. The Bible has help for us in leading lives that demonstrate growing maturity but it is Christ himself who saves us and empowers us to live.

Probably the most important role of the Bible is that as we read it or meditate upon its truth in either private or public worship the Holy Spirit illuminates the divine truth and enables us to meet Jesus Christ.

For some forty years my wife and I have followed the daily Bible portions supplied by Scripture Union, an international organization that promotes daily Bible reading.

1. John R. W. Stott, *Christ, the Controversialist*, Wheaton, Ill.: Tyndale House, 1970.

The recommended way to approach the Bible is to pray: "Open thou mine eyes, that I may behold wondrous things out of thy law" (Psalm 119:18).

Then the Scripture for the day is read. First, one seeks to learn what the verses have to say in the original setting, and then to seek their meaning for our lives. It is amazing how frequently the Bible "speaks to one's condition." There is guidance and correction; there is something for the mind and heart that gives new impetus to live a life pleasing to God. How wonderful to be brought into communion with the living Lord himself. Soon we find ourselves confessing specific sins and seeking forgiveness. Then there flows from our inmost heart sincere thanksgiving for what God has done for us in Christ. Praise and worship follow naturally and inevitably.

We discover that Christ bears witness to Holy Scripture and Scripture bears witness to Christ. The Holy Spirit is the unique Illuminator. The printed words of Scripture enable us to understand the principle of the Word made flesh. Our Lord was the perfect expression (Word) of the Eternal God; the Word became flesh. As we commune with Christ in Scripture our enfleshed lives are transformed. This produces the vivid experience of growing in grace and in the knowledge of the Lord Jesus Christ.

Earlier we touched upon the idea that we ingest the Word of God as food. You will recall that when our Lord was tested by Satan on the Mount of Temptation he told his adversary, "'Man shall not live by bread alone but by every word that proceeds from the mouth of God'" (Matthew 4:4 RSV). Again and again the Bible authors employ the analogy that as food—milk, meat, bread—is needed for the body's nurture, even more truly is the Word of God necessary for our spiritual growth.

Babies eventually are weaned from their diet of milk, but some Christians, who ought to be teachers, still remain on a milk diet. They are unskilled in "the word of righteousness" because they have not grown.

"But solid food is for the mature, for those who have their faculties trained by practice to distinguish good from evil" (Hebrews 5:14 RSV).

It is normal for a child to grow. He moves from milk and pablum to solid food quite unconsciously as the processes of growth occur in his body. Even though the analogy of food is used in describing spiritual growth, we should not push the analogy too far. One moves from milk to solid food in the spiritual realm by conscious effort. The stunted believers in Hebrews 5 were forced back on a milk diet because of their apathy. Christians grow by active faith and there must be an ingestion of compatible food.

There is no indication in Scripture that there is a place for permanently immature, spoon-fed Christians. The goal of Christian maturity is ever before us. Dependent on Christ and guided by his Spirit, robust, self-reliant witnesses begin to emerge as they apply themselves to the word of Scripture.

In the same chapter of the Epistle to the Hebrews a solemn warning is given to those who lapse into apostasy instead of going "on to maturity." Thus Christian growth is not just an option. It is essential. There may be no easy way to spiritual maturity, but believers are surrounded by super-natural means of grace, especially the Word of God. Therefore no excuses are accepted for apathy.

One of the major New Testament passages on the role of Scripture in the maturing process is in St. Paul's second letter to Timothy, his son in the faith: "But as for you, continue in what you have learned and have firmly believed . . . and how from childhood you have been acquainted with the sacred writings which are able to instruct you for salvation through faith in Christ Jesus. All scripture is inspired by God and profitable for teaching, for reproof, for correction, and for training in righteousness, that the man of God may be complete, equipped for every good work" (2 Timothy 3:14-17 RSV).

The Scriptures, described elsewhere as the sword of the Spirit, can slash open our smug lives. There is a dynamism to the Bible which has a way of challenging us to better levels of living. We find positive *teaching* (in the faith) and a *reproof* when we are off base. When it comes to life practices, the Scriptures offer *correction* and *instruction*. To what purpose? "That the man of God may be complete, equipped for every good work."

As has been indicated earlier the Holy Scriptures always work in tandem with the Holy Spirit, who illuminates our minds and helps us comprehend the Word of God. The Scriptures never work in isolation.

It is possible for us to grow as Christians only as we are spiritually united to Jesus Christ. But the principle of growth in him is not automatic. Rather we grow as we give obedient heed to Scripture and are dependent on the concomitant instrumentality of the Holy Spirit.

Christian growth results from these God-ordained means of grace, but we are not left to fend for ourselves in isolation. As soon as we are born spiritually, we discover we have become a part of a wonderful family—the people of God. This is the proper habitat of the growing child of God and the subject of our next study.

6

Life Together

If I were to ask you to draw a picture of what comes to your mind when you hear the word "church," what image would appear on the test paper? I think most of us would draw a building with a steeple. Even if we know better, most of us associate the word "church" with the building in which we meet each Sunday. But the Bible gives no such definition.

In recent years a flood of new books dealing with the church, its nature and mission, has poured from Christian publishing houses. Some of these have been designed to promote church unity, some have been written to further the cause of specific churches, and more recently there has been an emphasis upon "body life" and the importance of the gifts of the Spirit. We must confine ourselves in this book to the function of the church in promoting our growth as believers.

The books have been written against a cultural background in America that is strongly individualistic. So much of our religious history concentrates on the rights and privileges of individual Christians that a concept of "life together" does not appeal to us.

Even from our colonial beginnings the strong forces of history favored "free churches," that is, churches free from any central ecclesiastical authority, such as many settlers had known in the countries from which they had emigrated. The Reformation marked the break with the highly structured Roman Church. Then Puritanism, originally a movement to purify the English church from unscriptural beliefs and practices and from the liturgical trappings of Rome, set in motion reforms in church polity. Thus our Scottish and Scotch-Irish ancestors developed Presbyterianism, elders supplanting bishops in church government. The Independents, who later became known as Congregationalists, went a step further and gave the authority of church government to the people of the local congregations. The Baptists, stressing their distinctive doctrine of believers' baptism, followed the Congregationalists in their concept of church order.

When these groups broke their ties with the mother country and settled in the New World the already strong feelings of independence waxed even stronger. There were other non-religious influences, of course, that helped develop the individualistic character of Americans. Typically, Americans admire the self-made man in business, believe in the free enterprise system, and place a strong emphasis on personal salvation. The convert is taught that he must accept Jesus Christ as his *personal* Savior.

This is no tirade against free churches, free enterprise or personal freedom. Besides, our commitment to Christ as Lord and Savior is a very *personal* matter. Rather, this is an attempt to describe our religious, social, and political heritage in very bold strokes. It points up the fact that we are a nation of individualists.

Yet the Bible stresses a principle that is foreign to our normal thinking. Our life in Jesus Christ is a corporate life.

Our individual gifts, ministries, and even our personalities find greater opportunities for expression and growth in the communal fellowship of the church. It is a God-ordained life of relatedness in Jesus Christ. Collectivism suppresses individual freedom to magnify the role of the state. But in the corporate life of the church one lives in family relationship, each member seeking to help the others.

It is encouraging to note that this concept of the corporate character of the church, the Body of Christ, is developing across the United States. But it is alien to the thought processes of our secular society.

One of the prominent metaphors employed by the New Testament writers to describe the concept of the church is that of the body. There are other biblical figures of speech used to describe the church, and we should give heed to them, but for the moment the organismic character of the church is best understood in the divinely inspired analogy of the body.

"For by one Spirit are we all baptized into one body . . . and have been all made to drink into one Spirit," writes St. Paul. "For the body is not one member, but many" (1 Corinthians 12:13-14).

The body, with its various members—eyes, ears, hands, feet—all work in harmonious relationship. So it is in the Body of Christ. In the diversity of gifts, the various members serve and help one another. "But God has so adjusted the body . . . that there may be no discord . . . but that the members may have the same care for one another" (1 Corinthians 12:24, 25 RSV). This concept of mutual care and support shows us the wisdom of God in arranging for us to grow and develop as believers within a caring community.

In discussing the various "gifts" (charismata), all of which are "inspired by one and the same Spirit, who apportions to each one individually as he [the Spirit] wills" (1 Corinthians 12:11 RSV), it is important to realize that the gifts are dispensed for the benefit of all members of the Body of Christ.

While an individual believer may earnestly desire the higher gifts, it is quite plain that the Spirit of God distributes the gifts as he chooses. It is not our present purpose to discuss the various kinds of gifts—such as faith, healing, working of miracles, etc.—but it is enough to declare that the Spirit-energized gifts enable believers to grow and help others to grow.

The idea of a solitary believer, united to Jesus Christ and filled with the Holy Spirit but not joined to a company of Christians, is never taught in Holy Scripture. The people of God as a company were chosen in Christ before the foundation of the world. God places a high value on the church. "Christ loved the church and gave himself up for her . . . that he might present the church to himself in splendor, without spot or wrinkle or any such thing, that she might be holy and without blemish" (Ephesians 5:25–27 RSV). What Christian would desire to remove himself from the divine provision which assures us of development and an ultimate destiny of perfection? It would be presumptuous, even blasphemous, for a Christian to think he could make it on his own.

The usual rejoinder of those who spurn the fellowship of the church is that those who make up the membership are so imperfect. Yes, that is true. All believers are in varying degrees of maturity. That is just the point. We need one another in the growth process. We are here to help one another. The church is not a place for us only to be "fed" but it is the primary base for learning to minister to others. We are to be "servants of Christ, doing the will of God from the heart, rendering service with a good will as to the Lord and not to men, knowing that whatever good any one does, he will receive the same again from the Lord . . ." (Ephesians 6:6–8 RSV).

One of the great secrets of Christian growth is learning to be a servant. When we learn that life consists of serving and not being served we have made a major step in growth. The towel is our symbol.

It is in the church that the gifts of apostles, prophets, evangelists, pastors, and teachers are placed. It is in the church that the gifts of the Spirit about which we hear so much today operate. These gifts, or charismata, are not for our own enhancement or benefit. What then is their purpose? To equip "the saints [believers] for the work of the ministry, for building up the body of Christ" (Ephesians 4:12 RSV). So the real task of "the ministry" is in the hands of the believers, not just the clergy, as we often inaccurately assume. So every Christian is involved in "building up the body of Christ." But there is more.

This building process is to continue "until we all attain to the unity of the faith and of the knowledge of the Son of God, to mature manhood, to the measure of the stature of the fulness of Christ" (Ephesians 4:13 RSV).

Thus we see that spiritual growth is a corporate enterprise. Christian growth is not attainable except in the company of other needy people, like us, in the church.

And "we are to grow up in every way into him who is the head, into Christ, from whom the whole body, joined and knit together by every joint with which it is supplied, when each part is working properly, makes bodily growth and upbuilds itself in love" (Ephesians 4:15, 16 RSV).

In the household of faith we are enjoined to "pursue what makes for peace and for mutual upbuilding" (Romans 14:19 RSV). There are no solo operations. We work together and for one another.

It has been pointed out before that "the supreme purpose of the church is not the evangelization of the world," as Ray

Stedman has put it.[1] God's great purpose is that his people "be conformed to the image of his Son." The Scriptures indicate that God "predestines" this goal for his chosen people.

Such growth takes time. There may be crises in our spiritual understanding but growth is a long process. Many become discouraged for they expect instant maturity.

Stedman, in *Body Life*, tells about the buttons that are circulating among Christians today with these letters printed on them: PBPGINTWMY. That means "Please Be Patient, God Is Not Through With Me Yet." The goal of complete perfection is not reached overnight but each believer in the community of the forgiven should be moving forward in faith.

As we contemplate life in the church, it may seem to limit us. We fear we may lose out somehow in enjoying life's best. Then, too, some of our fellow Christians are such bores. They are not our kind. Do we have to put up with such a scraggly lot of people? Besides they don't seem to grow. They just sit in the pew (as I do)—just sit there. Nothing seems to happen. No one is concerned about me. Hardly anyone spoke to me last Sunday. I've decided to skip church next Sunday and go to the beach. Nobody will miss me.

This desolate picture applies to many congregations, yet it is not God's purpose for his people. If we are displeased with this situation, God hates it even more than we do.

The Lord keeps his people in covenant fellowship by his Spirit and his Word. Thus there are two basic requisites for a worshiping, growing church:

1. *The Bible must be faithfully preached.* There are some who go so far as to recommend the elimination of the sermon in worship. Yet it is in the preaching of the Word

1. Ray C. Stedman, *Body Life*, Glendale, Ca.: Regal Books, 1972.

that we hear the voice of the Lord speaking to our hearts and minds.

2. *The sacraments (ordinances) must be properly administered.* Those of us in the free church tradition foolishly disregard the beauty of worship that still prevails in the older communions. Word and sacrament are both essential in Christian worship. Baptism and the Lord's Supper are divinely given signposts that direct us to Jesus Christ and his work on our behalf. Just as the Scriptures point to Christ verbally, so the sacraments do visually.

But we must not restrict our concept of the Supper to a memorial view. It is true that our Lord said, "Take eat: this is my body, which is broken for you: this do in remembrance of me" (1 Corinthians 11:24). It is a memorial to him. But it is much more. When the disciples celebrated the holy meal they would recall that Jesus had often eaten with publicans and sinners. Even more acutely they would remember the intimate fellowship they themselves had with him at table.

They would interpret the Supper both as a prophecy and a foretaste of the future messianic banquet and a sign of the presence of the mystery of the Kingdom of God in their midst in the person of Jesus. They would see its meaning in relation to his living presence in the church, brought out fully in the Easter meals they had shared with him.

This Supper in the presence of their risen Lord as their Host would recall afresh the messianic miracle of the feeding of the multitude and his words about himself as the bread of life, signs of his continued self-giving in the mystery of the Supper.

They would relive the sacrificial and paschal aspect of the Supper: the Messiah's fellowship with sinners which reached its climax in his self-identification with the sin of the world on Calvary.

There is a life-giving relationship of communion between the events and realities—past, present and future—symbolized by the Supper and those who participate in it. This communion is so inseparable from participation in the Supper that we can speak of the bread and wine as if they were indeed the body and blood of Christ.

In participating through the Holy Spirit in the body of Christ which was offered once-for-all on the Cross, the members of the church are stimulated and enabled by the same Holy Spirit to offer themselves in eucharistic sacrifice, to serve one another in love within the body and ultimately to the needy world.

The word "remembrance" refers not simply to man's remembering of the Lord, but also to God's remembrance of his Messiah and his covenant.[2]

Whatever the free churches have gained in being loosed from the shackles of inflexible ecclesiastical control, they have lost in an emphasis on the beauty of worship. Holy Communion should not be an adjunct to a preaching service. Preaching, praise in hymns and songs, prayer and the Eucharist are integral parts of a service of worship.

Baptism, too, is a church service. Without getting into the ancient controversy about infant versus believers' baptism, one must accord this initiatory rite an important place in worship.

Many Christians today have fled from the dullness of traditional churches and joined home Bible classes, small groups or house churches. Without detracting from the recovered sense of fellowship and Bible study that is relevant rather than perfunctory, there is a great danger if such groups develop an anti-church bias. Small groups conducted under the aegis of the church can add much to its vitality. But the church, whether its worship is stately or simple, is

2. Adapted from Ronald S. Wallace on the Lord's Supper. From *Baker's Dictionary of Theology*, edited by Everett F. Harrison. Copyright 1960 by Baker Book House and used by permission.

where the sacraments are administered, where proper discipline is (or should be) exercised, and the Christian faith is guarded against error.

This is not a plea for a clergy-centered structure. By all means, let us have a church where the gifts of all the members are exercised. Thus individual members can grow as well as the corporate body.

Admittedly we face many problems in our churches. Neither the efforts of church politicians to forge an ecumenism from the top down, nor sheer enthusiasm at the other end of the spectrum will restore life in them. This will come through a combination of several factors: sincere worship of God, including a proper observance of the sacraments, biblical preaching, an obedient walking in the Spirit by members of the Body who demonstrate Christ's beauty (the fruit of the Spirit) in their lives, recognizing the gifts of the Spirit, and performing good works both within the Christian community and in the world where we are to bear witness. About this we shall have more to say.

7

Maybe Not a Star, but a Thorn

Amy Carmichael was a talented British woman who devoted her life to missionary service. In South India she established the Dohnavur Fellowship for the purpose of rescuing children from being used as temple prostitutes by Hindu priests. After a fall in 1931, Miss Carmichael was crippled with arthritis. For the remainder of her life she was an invalid, bedridden for the best part of twenty years.

Here is an example of how God permits a choice witness to endure a life of suffering. Here one comes face to face with the mystery of pain. Strange as it may seem to us, Christian growth is sometimes promoted by such means.

New life in Jesus Christ does not mean an avoidance of pain or hardship. Evangelism that promises that accepting Christ means a life without tribulation distorts the truth of God. The Bible plainly teaches that believers will experience suffering.

Take the example of Job, who lost his children and possessions, whose wife gave him no support, whose friends offered their gratuitous criticism and advice. The book of Job is a lengthy study of the problem of suffering.

In spite of his persistent prayer for relief, the Apostle Paul also had to endure his "thorn" in the flesh. He did not experience the healing he sought.

Suffering, it would appear, is an intrusion into God's perfect creation. Sickness, disease, and death are related to sin. It was not until Adam and Eve were tempted by the Adversary and the resulting Fall changed all human history, that pain and tribulation began to plague mankind.

The biblical answer to the mystery of suffering is complex. Our wounding and our healing both come to us from God. Our Lord, as the Suffering Servant, "was wounded for our transgressions, he was bruised for our iniquities . . . with his stripes we are healed" (Isaiah 53:5). So says the prophet Isaiah and the thought is echoed by Peter: "He himself bore our sins in his body on the tree . . . By his wounds you have been healed" (1 Peter 2:24 RSV).

When our Lord compassionately healed the blind, the deaf, and the lame, were these acts only attestations of his deity and limited only to the days of his earthly ministry? Or are these physical healings symbolic of that deeper healing of redemption?

These are profound questions that do not bring a unanimous reply from the church today. The wider aspects of suffering and healing are beyond the scope of this book. Even though the questions are tantalizing we must confine ourselves to suffering as it relates to Christian growth. I believe there is clear-cut biblical evidence that tribulation of all sorts is employed by God in the process of bringing us along on the road to maturity.

In the very epistle of Peter that tells us that by Christ's wounds we are healed, there is also this declaration:

"But the God of all grace, who hath called us unto his eternal glory by Christ Jesus, after that ye have suffered a while, make you perfect [mature], stablish, strengthen, settle you" (1 Peter 5:10).

True faith that wrestles with the problem of suffering does not receive a glib answer nor a justification of God's ways. That is what we learn from Job's experience. Paul was given a little more light on his predicament:

"And lest I should be exalted above measure through the abundance of the revelations, there was given to me a thorn in the flesh, the messenger of Satan to buffet me, lest I should be exalted above measure" (2 Corinthians 12:7).

There has been much speculation about the precise nature of Paul's thorn. Was it an eye affliction? His shortness of stature? Some chronic bodily affliction such as dysentery? No answer is given, and I suspect, this was in the plan of God. The thorn is a symbol of any sort of disabling affliction—physical or otherwise.

The important aspect of the account is that the suffering came to Paul from God (even though Satan was the messenger boy). Furthermore, the Lord took time to tell Paul that there was purpose in his suffering and that it was for his own good. "My grace is sufficient for thee," the Lord tells Paul. "My strength is made perfect in weakness" (2 Corinthians 12:9).

Paul gets the lesson. There is no masochism in his comment even though it is paradoxical for a human being to enjoy suffering. Paul says:

"Therefore I take pleasure in infirmities, in reproaches, in necessities, in persecutions, in distresses for Christ's sake." What a wide range of difficulties seems to be related to the thorn.

Paul concludes by making another paradoxical statement: "For when I am weak, then am I strong" (2 Corinthians 12:10).

But Scripture gives us further enlightenment on the role of tribulation and suffering in our character development. The basic teaching is found in the Epistle to the Hebrews. In the opening verses of chapter 12 our attention is directed to the example of Christ "who for the joy that was set before him endured the cross. . . ." The perfect Son of God recognized that there was purpose in his suffering. His was not a stoic enduring of pain but he entered into the experience, recognizing that there was meaning in the will of God.

Against this background the writer to the Hebrews quotes a passage from Proverbs:

"'My son, do not regard lightly the discipline of the Lord, nor lose courage when you are punished by him. For the Lord disciplines him whom he loves, and chastises every son whom he receives'" (Hebrews 12:5, 6 RSV).

Only those who have legitimate claims to membership in the family of God are entitled to discipline. God's purpose in chastising, or disciplining us is "for our good, that we may share his holiness" (Hebrews 12:10 RSV).

That it is perfectly normal to suffer pain is clearly stated. This is no mysterious rite wherein flagellation or self-inflicted pain yields a distorted pleasure.

"For the moment all discipline seems painful rather than pleasant; later it yields the peaceful fruit of righteousness to those who have been trained by it" (Hebrews 12:11 RSV).

Early in the history of the church the apostles understood this lesson when they gave their testimony, "rejoicing that they were counted worthy to suffer shame for his name" (Acts 5:41).

John Nelson Darby, pioneer teacher of the Brethren movement in Great Britain, illustrated the principles of God's purposes in perfecting his people by the story of a stone mason.

A huge stone is hewed out of a quarry and set aside by the workman for his purpose. With a definite image in mind, the workman chips away at the stone until he shapes it exactly as fits his plan. So God knows what our image will be and he takes whatever means are necessary in the conformation process.

Out of her own crucible of affliction, Amy Carmichael wrote feelingly about God's discipline. One of her most poignant poems is called "No Scar?".

Hast thou no scar?
No hidden scar on foot, or side, or hand?
I hear thee sung as mighty in the land,
I hear them hail thy bright ascendant star,
Hast thou no scar?

Hast thou no wound?
Yet I was wounded by the archers, spent,
Leaned Me against a tree to die; and rent
By ravening beasts that compassed Me, I swooned:
Hast thou no wound?

No wound? no scar?
Yet, as the Master shall the servant be,
And pierced are the feet that follow Me;
But thine are whole: can he have followed far
Who has nor wound nor scar?[1]

Job rose to great heights of spiritual understanding as he was undergoing his test of faith when he cried, "*when* he hath tried me, I shall come forth as gold" (Job 23:10). This recalls a story told by Miss Carmichael:

"The eastern goldsmith sits on the floor by his crucible. 'How do you know when it is purified?' we asked our village goldsmith. 'When I see my face in it,' he answered."

Sometimes Christians seem to go for years without reverses. Just when it would appear that they have had an unfair advantage through the forbearance of the Almighty, suddenly they find themselves beset by financial reverses, domestic difficulties, or serious illness. It is then that those

---

1. Amy Carmichael, *Toward Jerusalem*, Fort Washington, Pa.: Christian Literature Crusade, 1936.

in affliction are apt to ask the question, "Why?" Or a variant is "Why me?"

Helmut Thielecke, the gifted German theologian and preacher, declares that asking why is not the pertinent question. The proper one, he says, is "To what end?"[2] There is a self-centeredness about the question, "Why?" It seems to imply that pain is purposeless. Instead the man of faith recognizes that God has his sovereign purposes in our lives.

When we face crises we should not panic. Rather we must be aware that God is at work. It is true that a crisis makes us uncomfortable but the Lord Jesus becomes our teacher beyond where we are comfortable. Crisis clarifies the issues of the heart and reveals our need for mercy, forgiveness, and healing.

Perhaps we come closer to understanding the mystery of suffering if we hearken to the song of Hannah: "The Lord kills and brings to life; he brings down to Sheol and raises up. The Lord makes poor and makes rich; he brings low, he also exalts" (1 Samuel 2:6, 7 RSV).

In the Lord's own words, he likens our life to a branch of a vine. The imagery is clear. A branch has no life in itself unless it abides in the vine. But the analogy goes further. Sometimes branches have to be pruned. "Every branch that does not bear fruit, he prunes that it may bear more fruit" (John 15:2 RSV). If we are stopped in our tracks by some crisis it is very comforting to know that the Master Gardener our God and Father wants to see more fruit in our lives. There is cause for rejoicing when we realize we are being pruned by a wounded hand. The Gardener is never closer to us than when he is pruning the branches.

Sometimes suffering may be visited on a Christian be-

2. Helmut Thielecke, *Out of the Depths*, Grand Rapids: Eerdmans, 1962.

cause of sin in his life, but we do well not to judge any fellow believers who are experiencing pain or grief. This was the fearful error of Job's comforters. However, the case of the man in the Corinthian church who had an incestuous relationship with his mother-in-law is quite another story. The Apostle Paul upbraids the church for its tolerant attitude toward such blatant sin and he urges the Corinthians "to deliver such an one unto Satan for the destruction of the flesh, that the spirit may be saved in the day of the Lord Jesus" (1 Corinthians 5:5). There is a place for church discipline and it is a perilous thing to refuse to take action against open sin. Perhaps the failure to discipline members of the church is one reason there is such barrenness and lack of power in our local fellowships.

But let us not confuse such situations with the normal experience of believers. In the Epistle to the Romans, the Apostle Paul writes: "Let us even exult in our present sufferings, because we know that suffering trains us to endure, and endurance brings proof that we have stood the test, and this proof is the ground of hope" (Romans 5:3–5 NEB).

This same note is echoed in the Epistle of James: "Consider it pure joy, my brothers, whenever you face trials of many kinds, because you know that the testing of your faith develops perseverance. Perseverance must finish its work so that you may be mature and complete, not lacking anything" (James 1:2–4 NIV).

We can be glad that the Lord has enough interest in us to work in us to develop our spiritual maturity. We must learn this with a spirit of humility from the Lord Jesus himself: "Learn of me; for I am meek and lowly in heart: and ye shall find rest unto your souls" (Matthew 11:29).

We can react to suffering in different ways. We can shrug off the situation, secretly rebelling against our Lord's loving authority. We can be despondent, drenching ourselves with the tears of self-pity. Or we can listen to what C. S. Lewis calls pain: God's megaphone. Is God shouting something he wants you to hear?

Christians are likened to earthen vessels. But these clay vessels contain new life in Christ. The excellence is not ours but belongs to God. "For while we live we are always being given up to death for Jesus' sake, so that the life of Jesus may be manifested in our mortal flesh" (2 Corinthians 4:11 RSV).

While the ultimate goal is that God will make us mature by conforming us totally to the image of his Son, it is possible for us even now to demonstrate some measure of maturity.

Let us join with Peter in his benediction: "The God of all grace, who hath called us unto his eternal glory by Christ Jesus, after that ye have suffered a while, make you perfect, stablish, strengthen, settle you" (1 Peter 5:10).

This chapter cannot be concluded without mentioning the fact that both suffering and healing come from God. We use the Scriptures to our own destruction if we have an unbalanced view of these paradoxical forces. God is sovereign in his decisions. He declares: "I wound, and I heal" (Deuteronomy 32:39). He does not feel obliged to share all his counsel with us. That is why we often refer to the mystery of suffering. It may be difficult for those whose vocation is healing to realize that suffering also has an important place in the current program of God.

But he is also our healer. Indeed, there is no healing of our bodies or minds or souls apart from God. Physicians and those engaged in the healing arts only play an ancillary role. It is not primarily the medicine or the therapy. These are only instrumental. But ultimately healing comes from God alone.

Indeed it was to God that the Apostle Paul turned for the removal of his thorn. The fact that the Lord decided to refuse healing to Paul does not mean we should not always first turn to God for help. Graciously he may grant our petition but it is not healing on demand. Maybe our Lord can use the affliction more effectively than healing in bringing us to greater maturity. The promised total healing may be deferred until the day we shall be changed, conformed to the image of Christ.

8

For Wounded Psyches

Father John Powell, a perceptive author, teacher, and coun-selor, tells about a woman patient whom he had treated unsuccessfully. He felt angry and disgusted by his failure but nevertheless planned to resume counseling her.

When his classes at the university began in the fall, he received a phone call from his troubled friend. But instead of the "old neurotic whine, the same indecision, the same egocentricity" he expected to hear in her voice, he sensed there was something different about her. He had to ask several times, "Who is this?"

To his amazement the voice on the other end of the phone said she did *not* want an appointment. She was just calling to thank him for the patience and help he had given her over the last three years.

I couldn't believe what I was hearing. There was all the reso-nance of sincerity, but such abrupt personality changes just do not happen in real life. So I said: "You're different, aren't you?" And she replied: "Oh, yes!"
"What happened?"
"I met Jesus Christ."
"You what?"

"I met Jesus Christ. Before this I knew about Him, but now I know Him."

"If you tell me that you have had a vision. . . ."

"No, no vision. But I did meet Jesus Christ."

"I don't know whether you want to see me or not," I replied, "but I want to see you."

When she came to my office, my eye confirmed what my ear had led me to suspect. This was a "healed" person. I do not mean to detract one iota from the contribution they make to the lives of wounded human beings, but clinical psychology and psychiatry must not be allowed to pose as saviors or redeemers. Therapy can never be a substitute for a life of faith. I knew, from my training in psychology, that no reputable therapist could ever promise this kind of "cure", this new "wholeness." There is no plastic surgery to remove the psychological scars that all of us bear to some extent. By supportive psychotherapy we can be comforted, and by reconstructive psychotherapy we can be somewhat readjusted, develop new coping mechanisms, but . . . we cannot be healed or cured. This woman, seated before me, expressing gratitude and claiming to have met Jesus Christ was "healed." She knew it, and I knew it.[1]

This story highlights the problem of the relationship between spiritual maturity and emotional maturity. Perhaps it is in this area that we find types of suffering that are either self-imposed or at least buried in the complex recesses of human personality. It is not only for our bodies but for our emotions that we need the healing power of Jesus Christ.

The examples of the problem are manifold: I personally know literally thousands of Christians, mostly those in the conservative segment of the church. Through the years, I have known many who were regarded as leaders in the religious community but in private life their behavior has

---

1. Reprinted from *He Touched Me* by John Powell © 1974 Argus Communications. Used with permission from Argus Communications, Niles, Illinois.

often been unbelievably immature and unacceptable. Some were short-tempered, some were greedy for money, power, place or other illegitimate goals. Others have developed fear or depression which, though short of being pathological, marks the pattern of their lives.

Admittedly all Christians fall short of what they should be. Our Lord recognized this great truth when he declared: "So you also, when you have done all that is commanded you, say, 'We are unworthy servants; we have only done what was our duty'" (Luke 17:10 RSV).

One dare not be judgmental in appraising the behavior or works of one's fellows. It is easy to fall into the trap of unconsciously setting up our own conduct as the norm that others should follow. What arrogant spiritual pride! And we are all guilty of this, whether we admit it or not. Paul gives us pertinent counsel: "Not that we venture to class or compare ourselves with some of those who commend themselves. But when they measure themselves by one another, and compare themselves with one another, they are without understanding" (2 Corinthians 10:12 RSV). There is only one against whom we can measure ourselves—our Exemplar Jesus Christ. Always we must confess that all have sinned and come short of the glory of God.

Nevertheless, the prevalence of emotional problems among Christians has assumed crisis dimensions. Most pastors spend more than half their time counseling individual members or families. While I have not conducted a scientific survey, I have interviewed ministers in various parts of the country. They agree on this point: A good fifty percent of church families have some sort of domestic difficulties. What a contrast between our profession of orthodoxy and the cluttered condition of our personal lives!

That Christians have emotional problems just as commonly as people who are secularly oriented is increasingly evident. I sometimes wonder if Christians, especially those reared in moralistic homes, do not have more problems than the general populace. No doubt believers are faced with value structures that seem unattainable for them. Some are filled with real guilt; others with false guilt because their understanding of God's grace is deficient. Somehow they have failed to accept experientially the forgiveness so generously offered to all.

I hesitate to criticize the orthodoxy of my childhood training, but it does seem to me that I was reared in an atmosphere where sound doctrine was the ultimate goal of the Christian faith. The "truth" was taught as though we were dealing with abstractions. What new vistas of understanding were opened to me when I first discovered Paul Tournier's *The Meaning of Persons!* Tournier showed me that so much of biblical truth deals with relationships—our relationship vertically with God and our horizontal relationships with our neighbors, fathers, mothers, brothers, sisters, husbands, wives. The Bible tells us about people in real life situations. Truth is presented in terms of how individuals react with one another or in their concern for a personal God.

It is encouraging that schools of Christian psychology like the Graduate School of Psychology at Fuller Theological Seminary, the Rosemead Graduate School of Theology, and other similar institutions are training practitioners of Christian counseling and offering ministerial students courses in pastoral counseling. Often the Reformed faith, as some present it, seems doctrinaire. Yet, ironically, the Christian Reformed Church has developed some of our finest Christian psychiatric institutions, and a number of excellent counselors are members of this Calvinistic denomination. Westminster Theological Seminary of Philadelphia has given the Christian world Jay Adams and his disciples. Dr. Martin Lloyd-Jones, noted London-based Welsh physician-expositor, who is committed to the Reformed faith, has written on *Spiritual Depression: Its Causes and Cure.*

Out of a Fundamentalist background have come Clyde Narramore, Henry Brandt, and Bill Gothard. Of course, nearly all the major theological seminaries of the main line denominations have taught courses in pastoral counseling for years.

All this is to emphasize that even the most biblically oriented Christians today recognize that Christians experience serious psychic maladjustments. Not all these schools or practitioners in the counseling field are agreed on basic philosophy or therapy but their very existence argues that there is a pressing problem in contemporary Christianity.

In view of all the Bible has to say about the need for as well as the means of spiritual growth, what do we say about the lack of emotional growth of so many believers? Jay Adams particularly emphasizes the need for using the Scriptures in counseling.[2] He takes a dim view of Freudian and neo-Freudian psychoanalysis as well as behaviorism and existentialist psychiatry.

It is far beyond the scope of this book to attempt to assay the conflicting claims of various schools of psychiatry and psychology. But the Bible and counseling therapy have this in common: concern for human behavior.

Secular psychiatry, and Freud in particular, revealed that human beings possess an unconscious as well as a conscious mind. To this writer it appears that in the psyches of all men—unregenerate as well as regenerate—there is a fearfully complex mixture of conscious and unconscious factors. There seem to be hidden fears and tensions that contradict all that should characterize Christian behavior. Even Jay Adams and others who place complete confidence

2. Jay E. Adams, *The Use of the Scriptures in Counseling*, Philadelphia: Presbyterian and Reformed Publishing Co., 1975.

in "Bible therapy," stress the need for counselors who follow proper, i.e. biblical, guidelines.

The Bible seems to address itself to sentient individuals who bear full responsibility for their conduct. I have met several people who have been gripped by serious psychic or emotional problems, yet when they took the step of trust in the Lord Jesus, there were almost immediate remissions of their ailments. One woman, in particular, comes to mind since she is a radiant, effective Christian today. In her case psychiatry had failed, but the presence of Jesus Christ in her life now is plain to see. She does not have to tell you that she is a new creation.

In most cases, however, the mediation of a counselor is needed to help the person in trouble. Most of us seem incapable of receiving the healing that Jesus Christ offers. How often we have ears and hear not and eyes and see not.

Thus in the area of behavior that is motivated by unrecognized forces within us, Christian counseling is a legitimate, yes an essential, ministry within the household of faith. Ultimately though, each person must "give account of himself to God" (Romans 14:12). We can not cop a plea of insanity or neurosis. For in God's judgment hall even ignorance is sin.

Secular psychiatry that excuses aberrant or anti-social conduct on the basis of deterministic forces does not harmonize with biblical teaching about personal responsibility.

Someone may say that we are the victims of forces we do not control, such as our own sinful nature, but this is a specious argument, for God has amply provided forgiveness through Christ's sacrificial death on our behalf. Sinners we are, by birth and practice, but *there is a way of escape* from the universal condemnation of all men.

In the general confession in the Book of Common Prayer, it is stated eloquently:

"Almighty and most merciful Father; We have erred, and

strayed from thy ways like lost sheep. We have followed too much the devices and desires of our own hearts. We have offended against thy holy laws. We have left undone those things which we ought to have done; And we have done those things which we ought not to have done; And there is no health in us. But thou, O Lord, have mercy upon us, miserable offenders. Spare thou those, O God, who confess their faults. Restore thou those who are penitent; According to thy promises declared unto mankind In Christ Jesus our Lord. And grant, O most merciful Father, for his sake; That we may hereafter live a godly, righteous, and sober life, To the glory of thy holy Name."

Jesus Christ saved us totally; "holistically," if you will. In trying to resolve the problem of spiritual versus emotional growth, I think we must insist that salvation includes more than our "souls." It involves our emotional and physical life, too. There are past, present, and future tenses of salvation. It is evident that it will not be until the consummation of the divine redemptive program that we will be provided with imperishable bodies. The growth of our inward life is a lifetime process. But is it not also true that the Christian who walks with God and is benefitting from the means of grace may have improved physical and psychic health?

I know that some are called to demonstrate the grace of God by enduring suffering but that does not seem to alter the general principle. Also I am aware that a delivered alcoholic may die of cirrhosis of the liver even though he has found peace in Christ.

We live in a complex world. Each person has varying genetic influences, and environmental factors are never the same for even two of us. There are wide variations in our temperaments. Some are quiet and introverted; others are spirited extroverts. Think of the different personalities of children within the same family. Some of us are under-

privileged and some overprivileged. Yet God offers salvation
to all. The possibility of living a fruitful life is available to
every believer. Counselors may have to work painstakingly
to uncover the factors which inhibit emotional growth. But
growth in Christ is based on the premise that we have been
made new creations.

One of the difficulties of dealing with what we call emotional maturity is that there are no universally recognized
standards for being "normal." Would not Jeremiah or Amos
be regarded as kooks if they were judged by contemporary
mental health criteria? Perhaps we get hung up on the
jargon of psychiatry and do not sufficiently recognize that
Christian faith is a great source of emotional health.

Because we are made in God's image and because Christ
died on the Cross, we can be assured that we have great value.
This give us a balanced sense of self-worth that is not a sick
form of egocentricity. The gospel reaches out to everyone, no
matter how badly battered. For such a one Christian hope
can replace self-doubt and dark depression.

When I first came to a realization that I had been redeemed
by Christ, I recognized immediately that I possessed a new
sense of purpose. This is related to the sense of vocation that
is uniquely Christian. We are called by God to serve in our
respective areas of service, whether "secular" or "sacred."
The division between secular and sacred no longer applies,
for it is better to serve as a carpenter if that is our calling than
in the pastorate because it pleases the vanity of a family. God
uniquely bestows distinctive gifts on all of us. It is healthful
to know what these gifts are and then employ them with
confidence. Thus we shall be freed of our innate self-centeredness and neurotic preoccupation with self.

The lonely and estranged person can be delivered from the
bondage of alienation in the fellowship of the Christian
church. Despite the criticism that is constantly leveled at the
church, one can find loving friends there as in no other

human agency. Regardless of the psychodynamic forces that have shaped our lives or the damage from known or unidentified traumas, we can find healing in the wide-ranging invincible grace of God.

Surely life is full of conflict. The warfare never ceases. Our growth is challenged by those implacable foes: the world, the flesh, and the devil. With these contrary forces we shall deal next. Let the love of Christ cast out our fears and heal our wounded psyches as well as our souls.

Christus Victor!

9

Enemy Troika

The story that Martin Luther threw an inkpot at Satan probably is apocryphal. Many people today are amused by this story. In fact, they feel that the whole idea of the existence of a devil is ludicrous, that it is mere medieval superstition.

Yet Satan is a real personality. His part in the drama of redemption began in Eden and continues throughout redemptive history, including his temptation of Jesus Christ. Consider also how central this statement is to the crucifixion:

"For this purpose the Son of God was manifested, that he might destroy the works of the devil" (1 John 3:8).

Has the biblical teaching about Satan any relationship to the subject of this book? Do Christians today actually have encounters with the devil?

We must answer "Yes" to both these questions. Satan is the initiating leader in the ancient troika of foes actively opposed to Christian growth: Satan, the world, and the flesh. Or as we know it better: the world, the flesh, and the devil. A passage in Ephesians brings the three enemies together in a single reference:

"And you hath he quickened, who were dead in trespasses and sins; Wherein in time past ye walked according to the course of this world, according to the prince of the power of the air, the spirit that now worketh in the children of disobedience. Among whom also we all had our conversation in times past in the lusts of our flesh, fulfilling the desires of the flesh and of the mind; and were by nature the children of wrath, even as others" (Ephesians 2:1-3).

While one would desire that the main thrust of this book be directed towards the positive elements that promote Christian growth, it would be irresponsible not to point out that Christian pilgrims inevitably encounter opposition on the pathway of spiritual progress. The very strategy that we employ in dealing with our common foes is pertinent to growth. Certainly grace is greater than our sin. In Christ we can overcome the world, the flesh, and the devil. Let us deal with Enemy No. 1 first.

The superstition that the devil has horns, cloven hoofs, a tail, and an odor of brimstone must have been concocted by the old arch-deceiver himself. Satan is a master of the counterfeit and it is in line with scriptural teaching to think of him not only as a roaring lion, but also as an "angel of light."

"Our warfare is not with flesh and blood, but against spiritual wickedness in the heavenly places, against the rulers of this darkness," Luther declared, quoting Ephesians 6:12. "Let us then stand firm and heed the triumph of the Lord. Satan is fighting not against us, but against Christ in us. . . ."[1]

The father of Protestantism was better informed about Satan than most of us today. For example, if the proverbial man in the street were asked today about Satan, he would probably deny his existence or would humorously dismiss

1. Roland H. Bainton, *Here I Stand,* Nashville: Abingdon Press, 1950.

the subject with Flip Wilson's line, "The devil made me do it."

Some hint of the cosmic influence of Satan can be gathered from the colloquy in the book of Job between the Lord, accompanied by "the members of the court of heaven," and Satan. When the Lord asked Satan where he had been, the adversary replied blithely: "'Ranging over the earth . . . from end to end'" (Job 1:6, 7 NEB). From this we can infer that Satan has access to heaven. At the Temptation "once again, the devil took him [Christ] to a very high mountain, and showed him all the kingdoms of the world in their glory. 'All these,' he said, 'I will give you, if you will only fall down and do me homage [worship me].'" (Matthew 4:8, 9 NEB).

To remove the concept of a personal devil from the fabric of Christian faith is to nullify a central motif of the Holy Scriptures. No condescending ridicule can drive away the essential truth of Satan's reality, his personality, his active role, or his ultimate destiny.

Even though Satan is an implacable foe, primarily of Christ and derivatively of Christ's followers, it should not be assumed that Scripture portrays a dualism of equal forces of good and evil. Even though the warfare between God and Satan is graphically presented, there can be no doubt that God is ultimately, totally in control, and Satan, a "deteriorated creature," has limited powers and ultimately will be banished. Since his defeat at Calvary by Christ's death, he only reigns as the usurper "god of this world."

It is true that he is revealed as our "accuser," but his activities against the people of God are those of a defeated enemy staging a strategic withdrawal. The decisive battle of the great campaign has been won. "Having spoiled principalities and powers, he [Christ] made a shew of them openly, triumphing over them . . ." (Colossians 2:15).

But just how does Satan assail Christians today?

The idea of dealing with him is bizarre to most contemporary minds. Somehow the opposition of Satan to our growth as Christians seems remote and intangible. When Satan tempted Eve, he insinuated doubt into her mind, questioning God's commandment. He works still in the area of our thought processes and our emotions.

The devil had the capacity to control the personality of even such a devout follower of our Lord as the Apostle Peter. When the impulsive disciple rebuked Christ for announcing his forthcoming death, "Be it far from thee, Lord: this shall not be unto thee" (Matthew 16:22). Jesus quickly turned to Peter and said: "Get thee behind me, Satan: thou art an offense unto me: for thou savourest not the things that be of God, but those that be of men" (Matthew 16:23). On another occasion Christ told Peter that Satan had desired to have him but that he had prayed for him.

The point of these instances is that Satan was actively opposing the redemptive program of God and as the adversary he did not hesitate to oppress, obstruct, or attack even the apostles

Even as Jesus Christ is truth incarnate, Satan is a liar from the beginning. This description comes from the Lord Jesus himself: ". . . for he [the devil] is a liar, and the father of it" (John 8:44). In another place the Apostle Paul explains that the devil uses his own agents to promulgate false doctrine. The Corinthian church is told: "Such men are sham-apostles, crooked in all their practices, masquerading as apostles of Christ. There is nothing surprising about that; Satan himself masquerades as an angel of light. It is therefore a simple thing for his agents to masquerade as agents of good" (2 Corinthians 11:13, 14 NEB).

The Apostle Paul told the believers at Ephesus: "Put on all the armor which God provides, so that you may be able to stand firm against the devices of the devil. For our fight is not against human foes but against cosmic powers, against the authorities and potentates of this dark world, against the superhuman forces of evil in the heavens" (Ephesians 6:11, 12 NEB).

Thus Christians have full protection against such a formidable enemy. The armor of God includes the belt of truth as part of the panoply. The "sword of the Spirit" is the Word of God. Earlier we have noted that we are dependent for growth on absorbing Holy Scripture and "walking in the Spirit." Here we see that the Spirit and the Word are always used together. Our offensive weapon, or sword of the Spirit, is the Word of God. Let us not be paranoid about Satan. Rather let us wield the sword of the Spirit and rest in the grace of God.

Our second enemy is "the world" but we must be sure we know what that means.

One of our friends visited Grand Canyon for the first time. She was overwhelmed by the beauty and grandeur of this great spectacle of nature. As she stood on the canyon rim admiring God's creative handiwork, the thought came to her that the Almighty had pleasure in his own creation and found it good. Thus she was enjoying the same world that the triune God had made and enjoyed long before she was able to share the same beauty.

The world that God created he called good. We can still admire the goodness and perfection of God's world—fleecy clouds, blue skies, sunsets and sunrises, the majesty of mountains and sea, the fruitfulness of field and forest. Even more precious aspects of the goodness of creation are the gift of human love, an aesthetic sense, and the inspiring achievements of our cultural heritage.

The principal word translated "world" in the English New Testament comes from the Greek word which conveys the idea of an orderly and harmonious universe. But the same Greek word is employed in the New Testament in referring to the "world" of mankind, as in John 3:16: "For God so loved the world that he gave his only begotten Son. . . ." The key to understanding each citation is its context in Scripture.

There is a third use of the same word, which refers to the present distorted social order that exists in alienation from God. It is significant that Satan is called "the god of this world," the usurping sovereign who, as the enemy of God, has occupied the world and temporarily made it his dominion. He is the arrogant squatter who in the Temptation offered Christ all the kingdoms in this world. (He really did not have them to give.)

It is ironic that the original concept of an orderly universe has now come to mean "this present evil world" from which Christ has delivered us (Galatians 1:4).

Sophisticated modern men, steeped in the worldly philosophy of inevitable progress and man's innate goodness, have difficulty in realizing that our society has been polluted. Our worldly cultural values, by and large, are distorted. This is a world under condemnation, desperately in need of a divine Redeemer.

Whether modern man is willing to accept the concept or not, the Bible emphatically condemns the system of relationships, ideas, and values that are part and parcel of the "world" in this third sense. All of us reared in western culture unconsciously and automatically assume we live in a world that, while it is less than perfect, contains good as well as evil forces in more or less balanced proportions. The Bible makes no such admission. The Christian is commanded not to be conformed to the world (Romans 12:12).

James used strong language in describing the situation: ". . . Do you not know that friendship with the world is enmity toward God? Therefore whoever wishes to be a friend of the world makes himself an enemy of God" (James 4:4 RSV). We live in a world originally made to reflect God's glory but now the habitation of human beings in rebellion against God.

What can finite man do in such a grim situation?

It is comforting to know that "[Christ] delivered us [believers] from the dominion of darkness and transferred us to the kingdom of his beloved Son" (Colossians 1:13 RSV). Here are two co-existing kingdoms—Satan's, which keeps humanity in bondage, and, in contrast, Christ's new order which offers real freedom.

But what should be the Christian's relationship to the world order?

As we know, many well-meaning believers of past generations have sought to withdraw from the world to escape defilement, or the problems of life. David once cried out, "Oh that I had wings like a dove! for then would I fly away, and be at rest" (Psalm 55:6). But David was not a dove; he was a man.

Our Lord plainly indicated that the place of our witness is *in* the world even though we are not *of* it. In his high priestly prayer to the Father, the Lord said, "I do not pray that thou shouldst take them out of the world, but that thou shouldst keep them from the evil one. They are not of the world, even as I am not of the world" (John 17:15, 16 RSV).

We live in this present evil world because God has a purpose for us here. The one who loves the world has commissioned his disciples to "go into all the world to preach the gospel . . ." (Mark 16:15 RSV). But there is more than that. Christians are to be "salt" and "light" *in* the world. Salt is employed to preserve and to arrest decay. As "the light of the world" Christians are to let their "light so shine before men that they may see your good works and give glory to your Father who is in heaven" (Matthew 5:13, 14, 16 RSV).

To our materialistic generation, the injunction to love not the things of the world comes as an abrupt check. Loving *things* is related to covetousness and idolatry. This sin is the hallmark of our society. The believer who wants to grow dare not be trapped by the idolatry of materialism.

The faithful believer must not make the world his home. Rather he is to be a pilgrim and a stranger. In another analogy the Apostle Paul likens Christians to ambassadors representing the government of heaven. "So we are ambassadors for Christ, God making his appeal through us. We beseech you on behalf of Christ, be reconciled to God" (2 Corinthians 5:20 RSV).

Unbelievers have no problem of coping with this world: "You were dead through the trespasses and sins in which you once walked, following the course of this world, following [Satan] the prince of the power of the air, the spirit that is now at work in the sons of disobedience" (Ephesians 2:1, 2 RSV).

But the believer who wants to live in submission to the lordship of Christ will find the world a difficult and alien place. For serious disciples it offers a rocky path in the wilderness as well as suffering and trials. "In the world you have tribulation; but be of good cheer, I have overcome the world" (John 16:33 RSV). It is thrilling to know that the believing disciple whose trust is maintained in and by the Overcomer will himself be able to "overcome" the world. "And this is the victory that overcomes the world, our faith" (1 John 5:4 RSV).

It is abundantly clear that societal standards, even the most genteel, are false substitutes for the principles of Christ's Kingdom. Likewise the growing believer must be beware the "wisdom" of this world. With the constant barrage of messages hurled at us by the mass media, it is difficult to avoid conformity to the world, dominated as it is by covetousness and pride.

Immorality in politics, entrenched labor power blocs, dog-eat-dog business practices—all are a continuing scandal. Yet this is the place where the Christian is ordained to live, eating and drinking with sinners yet, like our Lord, morally separate. There is no place for other-worldly aloofness. Our place is right here.

Christians are the representatives of a new order, the Kingdom of God. In this capacity we not only have a responsibility toward individuals but are also concerned about effecting changes in the disrupted society. In so far as our resources permit, we will seek to establish enclaves of Kingdom order. By our very relationship to our compassionate Lord, we possess something of his heart in our concern for the poor and needy, orphans and widows. Using the legitimate means at our disposal, we will work against the forces of social, economic, and political evil. We shall be "zealous of good works."

Satan and the world are external enemies, but our most implacable foe, "the flesh," is internal. Right away we must understand that our "flesh" is not our body. The body is neutral and can be an instrument of good or evil.

"Flesh" is a sort of New Testament code word that refers to our old (Adamic) nature. This in no way implies that our fallen nature resides in our *bodies* any more than in our minds and hearts. The human personality is a psychophysical unity. Earlier in this book I have warned against the misconception that somehow the body itself is essentially evil.

There is a proper place for subduing the body as Paul asserts (1 Corinthians 9:27) but we should carefully differentiate between the body and "the deeds of the body" (Romans 8:13). It is our conduct or behavior, directed by the "flesh" that is branded as sinful. Thus eating and drinking are condoned, but not gluttony or drunkenness. God created us male and female but it is when sexuality, the gift of God, is improperly employed that it is called adultery or fornication. Sleep is legitimate. Too much is sloth. And there is no use blaming these sins on Satan.

Pogo, the perceptive possum of the cartoon strip, stated the problem concisely, "We have met the enemy and they is us."

Paul gives us a list of "the works of the flesh": "What human nature [the flesh] does is quite plain. It shows itself in immoral, filthy and indecent actions; in worship of idols and witchcraft. People become enemies, they fight, become jealous, angry, and ambitious. They separate into parties and groups; they are envious, get drunk, have orgies, and do other things like these" (Galatians 5:19-21 TEV).

It is because of the innate weakness of the flesh that the holy law of God could not provide salvation for us. It took God in Christ to accomplish for us "what the law, weakened by the flesh, could not do" (Romans 8:3 RSV). "The law is holy and the commandment holy, and just, and good" (Romans 7:12) yet it was unable to accomplish good because of the flesh, the limitations of sinful human nature.

Even the most devout Christians are torn by the constant civil war that rages within while Satan and the world storm the ramparts. Is there any way out of this strife?

First, we must review the basic facts. When we were baptized into Jesus Christ we were baptized into his death. Our old self was crucified so that we are no longer slaves of sin. Our identification with Christ in his death and resurrection is true for all believers.

In view of these facts, we are to consider ourselves "dead" to sin but "alive" to God in Christ. The promise then follows that sin will not have *dominion* over us. Note that we are not promised sinlessness.

The conduct of believers emanates either from the flesh or from the Holy Spirit who indwells us. We must distinguish between them.

On the positive side, we have been commanded to "walk in the Spirit." (The word "walk" always refers in Scripture to the bent of our behavior.) We are told that if we "walk in the Spirit, [we] shall not fulfil the lust of the flesh" (Galatians 5:16).

Since we are commanded to walk in the Spirit, that means we are addressed as responsible beings. It is by a conscious act of faith that we are to walk. Like the paralytic man of the parable, we hear the command to walk. The implication is that as we set our walking muscles in action, the Lord of life will provide the energizing power for us to move forward. Remember, our sins have already been forgiven, we have been given a new nature, and the Holy Spirit who indwells us will enable us to walk.

On the negative side, we must mortify the deeds of the body. That word "mortify" has an ominous sound, but we cannot dodge it. Note that we do not mortify our *bodies;* we mortify, or make dead, the *deeds* of the body.

Here is one of two Scripture references dealing with mortification: "For if ye live after the flesh ye shall die: but if ye through the Spirit do mortify the deeds of the body, ye shall live" (Romans 8:13; see also Colossians 1:5). Here again it is by the Spirit's energy that we deal negatively with deeds of the body since it is by his positive power that we are enabled to walk.

There seems to be confusion about the words "crucify" and "mortify." Some well-meaning persons use them inter-changeably.[2] But crucifixion is a past event, accomplished for all time by Christ. If we have been crucified with Christ, we are to consider this an accomplished fact and let it become operative in our conscious experience.

When one comes to Christ positive *faith* must be exercised. Yet there is also the negative aspect of *repentance,* which means turning one's back on the sinful course of the past. So we walk in the Spirit positively by faith. Negatively, by faith we mortify or starve out the sins we have been in the habit of committing.

2. There is one passage in Scripture in which the word "crucify" appears to mean the same thing as "mortify." "And those who belong to Christ Jesus have crucified the flesh with its passions and desires" (Galatians 5:24 RSV). Yet it should be noted that the past tense is employed and believers, by their relation to Christ, have shared his attitude toward their sin, the flesh, and the world. Perhaps some of the confusion regarding the usage of "crucify" is related to the King James Version rendering of Galatians 2:20: "I am crucified with Christ. . . ." Actually the RSV renders it correctly: "I have been crucified with Christ. . . ."

Do I need to press the point that many Christians have time for all sorts of activities which may be legitimate in themselves but because they are pursued relentlessly become the dominating factors in their lives? It is not very difficult to understand that some honestly confess, "I don't have much time for the Bible."

"For surely you know this: when you surrender yourselves as slaves to obey someone, you are in fact the slaves of the master you obey . . ." (Romans 6:16 TEV).

Some think that the way out of the trap we are considering is to be submissive to an external code. If you observe the don'ts of no movies, no cards, no drinking, no dancing, etc., you will be a strong Christian. Not true. The "code" has to be inside the heart and the Holy Spirit is the guide.

Actually such an approach is forbidden in Holy Scripture: "If you died with Christ to the basic principles of this world, why, as though you still belonged to it, do you submit to its rules: 'Do not handle! Do not taste! Do not touch!'? These are all destined to perish with use, because they are based on human commands and teachings. Such regulations indeed have an appearance of wisdom, with their self-imposed worship, their false humility and their harsh treatment of the body, but they lack any value in restraining sensual indulgence" (Colossians 2:20–23 NIV).

The code book approach denies the indispensable role of the Holy Spirit who creatively guides us to deal with the complexities of human experience. "If we live in the Spirit, let us also walk in the Spirit" (Galatians 5:25).

Besides the Spirit who will fill our lives and energize us, there is a provision that if we fail we may be restored to fellowship again. Confession of sin brings renewed forgiveness and cleansing. The Lord has thought of everything! What serenity of heart, what surging joy and contentment come to us when we make a habit of confessing our sins to a loving Father. This brings the knowledge that we are forgiven and cleansed immediately.

Here is the ultimate therapy for the believer who faces life realistically. When we candidly admit we have a proneness to sin, we are forced back into the dependence on Christ that is essential to growth.

Beyond the negative aspects of painful self-discipline are the positive graces and gifts that God bestows which contribute to the life abundant as we progress to full maturity.

10

The More Excellent Way

Recently I attended a memorial service for a woman who died in her late seventies after spending the last fourteen years of her life in a wheelchair. Until a stroke had deprived her of strength, she had been an active, vital woman. It was difficult to see her reduced to an almost vegetable existence.

But the hero of this story was her husband who cared for his ailing wife night and day, lifting her in and out of the wheelchair so that she could eat her meals, dressing and undressing her, bathing her and caring for her basic needs without complaint through the long years of her illness.

In all those years I do not recall hearing this faithful husband tell his wife that he loved her. Maybe he did, but his selfless care for her was a demonstration of love that went far beyond words.

There certainly is a place for verbal expressions of love, but the testimony of this man, which did not go unnoticed in the community where he lived, is that of love in action. The girls in the beauty shop, the waitresses in the restaurant, and all who had firsthand knowledge of this husband's faithful care of his wife were impressed.

Heretofore we have been examining the means of grace

God has provided for our growth as Christians and we have also been concerned with the forces which inhibit growth and how we may combat them.

But God also desires a response from us, even though we always remain his debtors. He has demonstrated his love in the supreme sacrificial act of sending his Son into the world to redeem us. While we were yet sinners, Christ died for us. This agape love of God has been poured into our hearts by the Holy Spirit. We now have the capacity to love.

"We love him, because he first loved us" (1 John 4:19).

How can there be any evidence of Christian life and growth in an individual who does not in some measure actively demonstrate love for God and love for the brethren?

The Bible does not define love in dictionary fashion, but in the classical passage in 1 Corinthians 13 we capture the spirit of the "more excellent way":

"Love is patient and kind; love is not jealous or boastful; it is not arrogant or rude. Love does not insist on its own way; it is not irritable or resentful; it does not rejoice at wrong, but rejoices in the right. Love bears all things, believes all things, hopes all things, endures all things" (1 Corinthians 13:4–7 RSV).

The Corinthians passage is not dealing with some esoteric or high-flown theories about Christian living. It meets us right where we live in our day-by-day contacts with other people. Here we are confronted by our own natural impatience and lack of consideration for others, our petty jealousies and resentments, our arrogance and vindictiveness. It is evident that unless love is poured into our hearts and we in turn exercise this gift of love in relation to others, we bear a testimony that convinces no one of our growth as believers.

Yet this passage also implies that the more we demonstrate kindness and outgoing love to people the more we are like God.

How many missionaries to different peoples and cultures

have demonstrated the love of God working incarnationally! A flood of memories rushes in on me: thoughts of faithful workers in New Guinea who loved the cannibals of that distant place; the representative of Christ who ministered to the prostitutes and lowly people of Korea (a whole church developed from a group of "honey bucket" men whose livelihood was going from house to house collecting human offal!); the English group who made a home for foundlings rescued from brothels. There is Mother Theresa who has given her life to the sick and the dying of Calcutta. The list of such heroes of the faith is endless. God's love working through human personalities underlines his redemptive purpose.

So much of the New Testament deals with the practical aspects of living. Hear the words of the Apostle Paul:

"Let love be genuine; hate what is evil, hold fast to what is good; love one another with brotherly affection; outdo one another in showing honor. Never flag in zeal, be aglow with the Spirit, serve the Lord . . . Contribute to the needs of the saints, practice hospitality. Bless those who persecute you; bless and do not curse them" (Romans 12:9-11, 13-14 RSV).

These words of encouragement seem to pour out of the Apostle's heart. He was not speaking in abstractions or pious platitudes. He had been through it all himself. He had been unjustly imprisoned, set at hard labor, beaten with many stripes, stoned, and suffered pain, weariness, cold and hunger. Yet he had reached a state of spiritual maturity that enabled him to "take pleasure in infirmities, in reproaches, in necessities, in persecutions, in distresses for Christ's sake" (2 Corinthians 12:10).

What a contrast to contemporary Christians sitting in comfortable pews as spectators rather than manning the battle lines as warriors in the ongoing warfare of the faith.

Our Lord has enjoined us to live triumphantly in the midst of the battle. "I say unto you, 'Love your enemies, bless them that curse you, do good to them that hate you, and pray for them which despitefully use you and persecute you . . . For if ye love them which love you, what reward have you?''' (Matthew 5:44, 46).

Actually, we struggle with the same problems as God's ancient people Israel. How difficult it must have been for them to obey the commandment: "Thou shalt love the Lord thy God with all thine heart, and with all thy soul, and with all thy might" (Deuteronomy 6:5). They were *commanded* to love God. They must have been as stumped by it as we are today. Love for God is more than an ephemeral emotion. It involves the mind, the heart, the will, the total strength of our being. This love is more than a spiritual high, a warm feeling, or a sentimental impulse. Our Maker has given us the capacity to respond to him and he holds us responsible to obey. We demonstrate our love for God not by mechanical religious ritual or mindless gazing into the infinite. Love is not the legalistic fulfilment of grim duty or suffering pointless penance but a submission to the lordship of Christ and an offering of ourselves in voluntary, helpful service to those in need.

The contemplation of God in Christ gives the Christian a likeness to God. "But we all, with open face beholding as in a glass the glory of the Lord, are changed into the same image from glory to glory" (2 Corinthians 3:18).

This loving attention to Christ enables us to grow. Thanks to the divine provision, our reponse causes things to happen inside us.

Like the husband who is concerned about pleasing his wife because he loves her, so the Christian must be concerned about what pleases God.

But you may say, "I find it difficult to love God," or, "How can I have enough love for God?" Every believer is stymied by such questions. But at this point we need not be concerned about the perfection of our love; we shall never attain that on earth. It is the direction of love that must engage our attention. As we walk with God in the Spirit our love will increase. We have a lifetime ahead of us to know him better.

But Jesus shows us that our love for God does not stand in isolation from our love for those nearest us in need—which I take to be the meaning of the word "neighbor." Loving God is, of course, "the first and great commandment." But Jesus continues; "And the second is like unto it, Thou shalt love thy neighbor as thyself. On these two commandments hang all the law and the prophets" (Matthew 22:38–40).

If we are dismayed by the command to love God, we may be overcome by the seeming impossibility of loving our neighbor (whoever he is) as ourself. Down deep in our hearts we know our most cherished idol is our own ego. We need no goading to love ourselves despite the repeated injunctions of popular psychologists. (There is a difference between self-love and self-acceptance.)

Nor can we cop out by asking the question the lawyer directed to Jesus: "And who is my neighbor?" (Luke 10:29). Jesus did not attempt to define "neighbor"; he recounted the story of the Good Samaritan who discovered the half-dead victim of a mugging and showed compassion toward him. It would seem that Christ was saying that our "neighbor" is any human being in need.

We must not deduce that humanitarian acts in themselves are enough. Love for God comes first. Our love for other human beings is second but love for God and man are now forever integrated.

Very pointedly the Apostle John tells us, "If a man say, I love God, and hateth his brother, he is a liar: for he that loveth not his brother whom he hath seen, how can he love God whom he hath not seen?" (1 John 4:20).

Perhaps we can understand how we can grow in understanding the principles of love if we give attention to these words of the Apostle in the same chapter:

"Dear friends, let us love one another, for love comes from

God. Everyone who loves has been born of God and knows God. Whoever does not love does not know God, because God is love. This is how God showed his love among us: He sent his one and only Son into the world that we might live through him. This is love: not that we loved God, but that he loved us and sent his Son as an atoning sacrifice for our sins. Dear friends, since God so loved us, we also ought to love one another. No one has ever seen God; but if we love each other, God lives in us and his love is made complete in us" (1 John 4:7-12 NIV).

The Lord earlier told his disciples that their love for one another was the greatest testimony they could give to the world.

The Body of Christ is ordained to be a true community of love. " 'A new commandment I give to you, that you love one another; even as I have loved you, that you also love one another. By this all men will know that you are my disciples, if you have love for one another' " (John 13:34, 35 RSV).

Both Old and New Testaments are replete with injunctions to love God and love those about us. The New Testament gives us fuller understanding of the dynamics of projecting divine love. The indwelling Holy Spirit enables us to love spontaneously and supernaturally. "If we live by the Spirit," says the Apostle Paul, "let us also walk by the Spirit" (Galatians 5:25). Love as a "fruit" of the Spirit is the first in a nine-fold cluster of graces that are consonant with Christian maturity and likeness to Christ. The late Bishop J. C. Ryle of Liverpool, has pointed out that humility and love are the graces men of the world can understand, even if they do not comprehend doctrine.

Walking in love is the primary evidence that a believer is maturing, but there are further responsibilities which we will examine next.

11

How To Please God

Irene Webster-Smith, a missionary to Japan, tells the story of how faith became a reality in the lives of the little Japanese girls who lived in her Sunrise Home.[1] Miss Webster-Smith had frequently stressed the significance of our Lord's word to his disciples: " 'If you have faith as a grain of mustard seed, you will say to this mountain, "Move hence to yonder place," and it will move; and nothing will be impossible to you' " (Matthew 17:20 RSV).

Sunrise Home was located at Akashi on the shores of Japan's Inland Sea. But a huge mound of earth—the children called it their "mountain"—cut off the view from the back window. The mound stood on property belonging to the city.

At first the children set at work with shovels to remove the "mountain" by their own efforts. But the work went slowly in the humid summer heat and the children's interest began to flag.

The kindly missionary suggested that they pray about the problem. Little Sacheko prayed: "Lord Jesus, last Sunday we heard in Sunday School that if we had faith as a grain of

1. Russell T. Hitt, *Sensei*, New York: Harper & Row, 1965.

mustard seed, we could remove mountains. Lord, help us remove our mountain."

Then Hanachan prayed, "You said we could move a mountain into the sea. Here the sea is just across the road. Will you please take our mountain and put it into the sea?"

Not long after this the children arose one morning to find their "mountain" was disappearing before their eyes. The city of Akashi had sent out workmen with shovels and picks who loaded the dirt into a truck and in several trips hauled it away for land fill. Before the day was over their entire "mountain" had been removed.

Even though love is declared "the more excellent way" as an expression of ongoing Christian witness, our Lord and the New Testament writers preferred to speak of faith as the operative word for describing life pleasing to God.

It is faith that brings us into saving relationship with God in the first place. ". . . By grace are ye saved through faith; and that not of yourselves: it is the gift of God" (Ephesians 2:8, 9). Our sovereign God has decreed that we receive the gift of salvation when we respond in faith.

Now just as our new being began by our faith response, so we proceed through our Christian life walking by faith. Such faith is not only mental assent; it is also an act of spiritual commitment of our total being—heart and mind and will. Thus it is not just agreeing intellectually with a creedal statement; it is full commitment to a person, the Lord Jesus Christ. That is the way we proceed in the Christian life. We learn that ". . . without faith it is impossible to please him [God]" (Hebrews 11:6).

This great principle of living by faith, required of all believers, is illustrated by the lives of the heroes of faith in Hebrews 11. Abraham demonstrated his faith by offering up his son Isaac. Moses showed his confidence in God by "choosing rather to suffer affliction with the people of God, than to enjoy the pleasures of sin for a season" (Hebrews

11:25). Strangely enough, Rahab the harlot, transcended her godless culture by receiving the spies of God's people. In all these cases faith is not a passive state; it is expressed in acts of reckless devotion.

When a poor Gentile woman, who had hemorrhaged for twelve years reached out and touched Christ's garment, she was healed instantly. She recognized who Jesus was and his great ability to heal. It was faith that impelled her to touch Jesus' garment. Then the healing came from him. And he tells her, "Daughter, thy faith hath made thee whole . . ." (Mark 5:34).

A recently published manual describes three levels of faith: *believing faith, trusting faith,* and *expecting faith.*[2] Accepting basic doctrinal truths may be described as "believing faith," which is essential but not sufficient. "You believe that God is one; you do well. Even the demons believe—and shudder" (James 2:19 RSV). "Trusting faith" goes beyond assent to doctrine to trusting one's life in God's hands. That is better but it is not enough. "Expecting faith" reaches out and looks to God to act.

Fortunately it is possible for our faith to grow. Paul commended the Thessalonians because "your faith is growing abundantly" (2 Thessalonians 1:3 RSV). If you feel your faith is weak, follow the example of the father of the epileptic boy. Jesus first told the distraught man: "'All things are possible to him who believes.' Immediately the father of the child cried out and said, 'I believe; help my unbelief!'" (Mark 9:23, 24 RSV).

Faith is our response to God's grace as our love is a response to his love. As we have dealings with God our imperfect faith will grow. Even the great Apostle Paul did not become a lion of faith overnight. He admits: "Yet, my

---

2. *Basic Christian Maturity,* a training manual developed by the Word of God Community, Ann Arbor: Word of Life, 1975.

brothers, I do not consider myself to have 'arrived' spiritually, nor do I consider myself already perfect. But I keep going on, grasping even more firmly that purpose for which Christ Jesus grasped me. My brothers, I do not consider myself to have fully grasped it even now. But I do concentrate on this: I leave the past behind and with hands outstretched to whatever lies ahead I go straight for the goal—my reward the honor of my high calling by God in Christ Jesus" (Philippians 3:12-14).[3]

Paul's honest declaration that he had not arrived spiritually offers encouragement to the rest of us who are all too aware of our faltering belief. It must be apparent though that our heartfelt attitude toward God has a direct bearing on how much we grow in our faith.

Not all Christians follow the example of Paul in admitting they have not reached perfection. I am always disturbed by the "super-spiritual" types who profess that they are *fully surrendered*. I think it is a perilous thing to declare too glibly that one finds himself doing the "perfect will of God." As far as I am concerned such expressions are inappropriate for any of us. At best we are unprofitable servants, and none of us is yet fully yielded.

Another response that bothers me is the individual who talks about his faith as if it were a self-contained entity. *My* faith in and of itself is meaningless. It is only as our faith is directed to God in Christ that it has meaning. Faith, in the biblical understanding of the word, is more than credence in propositions (though it certainly includes the concept). Faith ultimately is trust or confidence in a person—even Jesus Christ our Lord. Of course, genuine Christian faith involves belief in what God has revealed concerning his character and purposes. Faith involves the acknowledg-

3. J. B. Phillips, *The New Testament in Modern English*, New York: Macmillan, 1959.

ment that Jesus Christ was the promised Messiah and incarnate Son of God. There may be incipient faith where information about Jesus is incomplete. But true faith does not appear when Christ's deity is consciously denied. (See 2 John 7-9.) Related to this is the need for believing and obeying "the truth," as it is biblically defined. (See Titus 1:1; 2 Thessalonians 2:13; 1 Peter 1:22.)

God has performed his mighty acts of redemption in history. Thus there is an objective reality to the Christian faith. We accept the apostolic testimony of the New Testament. "We have not followed cunningly devised fables," as Peter declares (2 Peter 1:16). Thus our faith in God is more than a supposedly self-authenticating mystical experience. We accept the testimony of a God who cannot lie, knowing that our own emotional or experiential response cannot be trusted completely.

This is not to deny the wide variety of our spiritual experiences nor to deny the mystery of certain aspects of the way God makes himself known to us. Somehow God communicated with the pagan Abram in Ur of the Chaldees. Samuel heard the voice of the Lord as did Elijah and Elisha, Isaiah, Jeremiah, and a host of holy men and women.

But all subjective experience needs to be checked against what Peter calls a "more sure word of prophecy" (2 Peter 1:19). In the same context, the Apostle tells us how the Holy Scriptures were given by God: "Men moved by the Holy Spirit spoke from God" (2 Peter 1:21 RSV).

Where does faith come from? And how can we increase our faith?

There is no formal definition of faith in the Bible. Even the famous passage in Hebrews (11:1) tells us what faith does rather than what it is, according to the late Dean F. W. Farrar: "Now faith is being sure of what we hope for and certain of what we do not see" (NIV).

The basic Scripture passages dealing with the origin of

saving faith hark back to the beginning of the new life in Christ. Two portions in particular describe the role of faith in our coming to Christ in the first place.

First the long quotation from Romans 10:8–11; 13–15:

> . . . The word is near you, on your lips and in your heart (that is, the word of faith which we preach); because, if you confess with your lips that Jesus is Lord and believe in your heart that God raised him from the dead, you will be saved. For man believes with his heart and so is justified, and he confesses with his lips and so is saved. The scripture says, "No one who believes in him will be put to shame." . . . For "every one who calls upon the name of the Lord will be saved."
> But how are men to call upon him in whom they have not believed? And how are they to believe in him of whom they have never heard? And how are they to hear without a preacher? And how can men preach unless they are sent? As it is written, "How beautiful are the feet of those who preach good news!" . . . So faith comes from what is heard and what is heard comes by the preaching of Christ.

The late John Murray, noted Reformed scholar, declared that faith arises from the message proclaimed. In other words "there cannot be faith except as the gospel is communicated in proclamation and comes within our apprehension through hearing."[4]

The second passage that many quote in referring to the origin of faith is Ephesians 2:8: "For by grace are ye saved through faith; and that not of yourselves: *it is* the gift of God."

Some interpreters regard "faith" as the antecedent of "it." But in the total context of Ephesians 2:8 and 2:9 the thrust of the passage seems to stress that salvation is the "gift" referred to and that it is not achieved by works. In any case, "it is the voice of God that arouses; it is the power of God that gives

---

4. John Murray, *The Epistle to the Romans*, Grand Rapids: Eerdmans, 1965.

strength to act; it is the same power which makes provision for the need of the new life."[5]

The gospel or the word of Christ generates faith in the first place, but the continuing experience or practice of believing is shared by all who are in Christ and possess the life of God. There is a close relationship between the presence of the indwelling Holy Spirit and the ability or capacity to believe. Thus Christians early came to be called "believers." (The Greek noun for "faith" and the Greek verb for "believe" are from the same root.) The Holy Spirit within believers is the mark put on men only as they believe.

The Christian way is only possible for those who walk by faith and not by sight. As Leon Morris declares, "Christianity is more than a system of good advice. It not only tells men what they ought to do, but gives them power to do it."[6]

"My sheep hear my voice," the Savior said, "and I know them, and they follow me" (John 10:27). Following Jesus is the proper course for every Christian. It is impossible to please God or to demonstrate growth without the continuing attitude of faith.

This attitude of faith is described in the Old Testament as "trust." Long before the fulness of the New Testament revelation, Solomon declared, "Trust in the Lord with all thine heart; and lean not unto thine own understanding. In all thy ways acknowledge him, and he shall direct thy paths" (Proverbs 3:5, 6).

The Psalmist spoke in a similar vein: "Delight thyself also in the Lord; and he shall give thee the desires of thine heart. Commit thy way unto the Lord; trust also in him; and he shall bring it to pass" (Psalm 37:4, 5).

5. Francis Foulkes, *The Epistle of Paul to the Ephesians*, Grand Rapids: Eerdmans, 1963.
6. Leon Morris, "Faith," *The New Bible Dictionary*, Grand Rapids: Eerdmans, 1962.

Paul readily acknowledges "the life which I now live in the flesh I live by faith in the Son of God" (Galatians 2:20 RSV).

Faith is a key word of the New Testament. God provides initiating grace, but every believer must respond in faith and obedience.

"Faith means abandoning all trust in one's own resources. Faith means casting oneself unreservedly on the mercy of God. Faith means laying hold of the promises of God in Christ, relying entirely on the finished word of Christ for salvation, and on the power of the indwelling Holy Spirit of God for daily strength. Faith implies complete reliance on God and full obedience to God."[7]

7. Leon Morris, "Faith," *The New Bible Dictionary*, Grand Rapids: Eerdmans, 1962.

12

Faith in the Future Tense

Jean-Paul Sartre's play *No Exit* dramatizes the meaning-lessness of life for many of our generation. Like other secular existentialists, Sartre seems obsessed with this theme—the futility of existence. There is no escape for man.

Certainly this is an understandable diagnosis of the condition of a world in which there is so much anguish and alienation. The personal and social problems have never loomed so large. No wonder depression is the most prevalent emotional disorder. Escapist solutions like drugs and alcohol, gambling, shopping sprees, and sexual adventures, reflect the frenetic mood of a generation that concentrates on immediate gratification and self-fulfilment. It recalls the biblical description of a pagan world that is "without God and without hope."

Hope issues from biblical revelation and the comprehensive program of divine redemption. Only in the Christian faith and its forerunner, the faith of God's ancient covenant people, do we find the basis for a living hope that can transform our lives. Thus hope, like love and faith, is an essential element for growth.

Without the deep-seated confidence that a believer possesses in a sure future, an individual must escape into a fantasy world of his own design. Such a person can resort only to escapism or despair.

"Hope" is essentially a New Testament word but the concept exists in the Old Testament as well. The Hebrews trusted in a personal God and Ruler who loved his special people. He revealed his love and power in mighty acts, such as the delivery of the entire nation from Egyptian bondage through the Red Sea, and the long journey to the land flowing with milk and honey. Even though Israel disobeyed Jehovah and worshiped false gods, their loving Redeemer-God announced through his prophets that a Messiah-Deliverer would come and establish a kingdom that would never end.

It is because of what God has done in the past in preparing for the coming of Christ and because of what he has done and is doing now through Christ, that a Christian has confidence in what God will do in the future.

More precisely, Christian hope is related to the objective fact of the triumphant resurrection of Jesus Christ. "If in this life only we have hope in Christ, we are of all men most miserable," the Apostle Paul tells us (1 Corinthians 15:19). It is because of Christ's resurrection that every believer can look forward also to the future prospect of his own resurrection from the dead. Hope is thus faith expressed in the future tense.

A recent television program presented an interview with a prisoner facing a long period of incarceration. His interviewer asked him if he often had thoughts of escaping. Yes, indeed, said the prisoner, it was the dominating thought of nearly everyone in jail. Life was insufferable apart from a hope that one day there would be liberation—either through his own efforts or other means.

Scripture presents ordinary life situations, such as a farmer plowing the ground in hope of a future crop (1 Corinthians 9:10), as examples of confidence in ongoing providence. For our own sanity and self-understanding it is essential to recognize that there is a purposeful pattern to the daily flow of events. How much more soul-satisfying and exhilarating it is to realize that we are related to a sovereign, all-wise and loving Creator-Redeemer who has things under his ultimate control. Otherwise we are caught in a morass of meaningless and unrelated events.

The Christian hope is a sublime confidence in a living God who acts and intervenes in human life and can be trusted to implement his promises to us. This kind of hope does not depend on our individual temperaments nor upon circumstances. Rather it is a supernatural inner confidence generated in our hearts by the Holy Spirit.

There is a delightful twist on the word hope used in Paul's description of Abraham facing up to the impossible promise of God that Sarah would bear a son in her old age. "In hope he believed against hope, that he should become the father of many nations" (Romans 4:18 RSV). Sometimes our hope may be "against hope," that is, against reasonable expectations, but this spiritual grace arises in our hearts by the Holy Spirit's action. It becomes "an anchor to the soul."

Just as love and faith can grow, so our hope develops as we surmount the joys and sorrows of living. Here is the biblical progression: ". . . We rejoice in our sufferings, knowing that suffering produces endurance, and endurance produces character, and character produces hope, and hope does not disappoint us, because God's love has been poured into our hearts through the Holy Spirit . . ." (Romans 5:3-5 RSV). The Christian life is not static. The divine means of grace which we have been discussing in earlier chapters enables us to demonstrate a growing maturity in love and faith and hope. Likewise these same abiding qualities are themselves dynamic forces for further growth.

Contemplation of what has been accomplished in Christ is the sure course of attaining and maintaining hope. "For everything that was written in the past was written to teach us, so that through endurance and the encouragement of the Scriptures, we might have hope" (Romans 15:4 NIV).

Our possession of hope moves from privilege to responsibility as we minister to those who cross our path. There is no greater testimony to the world than the Christian who radiates love, faith, and hope. They may be invisible qualities yet they speak louder and more effectively than more conscious efforts at witness. Peter tells us to "be ready always to give an answer to every man that asketh you a reason of the hope that is in you with meekness and fear" (1 Peter 3:15).

So many times Christian friends ask me for tips on witnessing to others in one-to-one conversations. I nearly always reply that it is better if the other person asks the questions. But perhaps I can tell future inquirers that "questions from others will be forthcoming when your hope is showing!"

In earlier chapters of this book I have stressed that Christian maturity is measured by our becoming more and more like Jesus Christ. The ultimate goal is complete conformity to his likeness. Now we learn that hope is an integral part of this process: "Dear friends, now we are children of God, and what we will be has not yet been made known. But we know that when he appears, we shall be like him, for we shall see him as he is. Everyone who has this hope in him purifies himself, just as he is pure" (1 John 3:2, 3 NIV).

Life takes on a completely different hue when we can look to the future with full confidence that the best is yet to come. The message of this volume is summed up in a relatively obscure passage of Scripture:

"For the grace of God that brings salvation has appeared to all men. It teaches us to say 'No' to ungodliness and worldly passions, and to live self-controlled, upright and godly lives in this present age, while we wait for the blessed hope—the glorious appearing of our great God and Savior, Jesus Christ, who gave himself for us to redeem us from all wickedness and to purify for himself a people that are his very own, eager to do what is good" (Titus 2:11-14 NIV).

Thus the Christian lives in time, conscious that God has saved him for a purpose which involves living a life of purity and good works.

The Christian is buoyed up by the realization that Jesus Christ is coming back and will usher in his kingdom. This hope and expectation of the Second Coming must not give rise to an escapist preoccupation with the future. Rather the "blessed hope" should spur the believer on to greater zeal in good works.

"It was hope which kept Adoniram Judson at it, preaching every day for fourteen years in a Burma bazaar without seeing a single convert, and then saying, 'The future is as bright as the promises of God.' "[1]

God has done so much for us that we have no excuse for apathy, discouragement, sloth, or resignation to failure. We are engaged in a holy war, but our weapons and spiritual stamina are provided by God. If thus far you have not found the reason for a lack of growth, perhaps this question is in order: What place does prayer have in your life?

1. J. Sidlow Baxter, *Awake, My Heart*, Grand Rapids: Zondervan, 1960.

13

Approach the Throne with Confidence

One of the great saints of modern days was the late Dr. Northcote Deck, medical missionary to the Solomon Islands. I served with him on the American board of Inter-Varsity Christian Fellowship after he had retired from the field and was living in Toronto. Because we had similar Christian backgrounds and many common interests, we became good friends. I shall never forget an occasion when we met at a board meeting in Chicago and he told me he prayed for me every day. It is difficult to express how much that meant to me.

Not too many of us know much about prayer, yet it is high on the list of the factors promoting Christian growth. We know that we must love God and that we cannot please him without faith, but can any sincere believer fail to see that prayer is also essential to communion with God?

Rosalind Rinker, an author of many books on prayer, says: "I have discovered that prayer's real purpose is to put God at the center of our attention, and forget ourselves and the impression we are making on others."[1]

1. Rosalind Rinker, *Prayer: Conversing with God,* Grand Rapids: Zondervan, 1959.

Miss Rinker has stressed the importance of conversational prayer—that is, individuals in a group praying back and forth on a single subject. This develops a sense of the presence of God himself.

Perhaps many of us have memories of long, stilted prayers that completely bored us. I can still recall the smell of varnish on a wooden rocker where as a boy I kneeled during family devotions. I must admit candidly that these were not sessions in which my spirit soared in bliss.

But later when I began to perceive what God had done for me in Jesus Christ, I began to enjoy early Sunday prayer meetings with a group of young men. Nearly all the members of that group later entered some form of Christian work.

But why should prayer be so important in our growth? Are we not united to Christ, indwelt by the Holy Spirit, equipped with the Holy Scriptures, and in fellowship with other believers in the church? Are not these great gifts enough?

Spiritual growth is not automatic. God has ordained that, while his grace is sufficient for all our needs, it becomes a part of our experience as we exercise trustful, active faith in him. Even a millionaire has to write a check before his wealth can be made usable for daily needs.

The Lord has ordained the means by which we approach him. Remember, he is a loving, personal God who has not only given us natural life, but has also provided for our redemption. This means that we have become a part of the family. And he is our Father.

Jesus has given us the greatest insights on prayer. His emphasis was always on the Fatherhood of God. He also stressed that we are heard by God as persons when we come to him in prayer. We are not turning a prayer wheel for an impersonal force. We are communing and conversing with the head of the family. We can be at home in his presence.

There is a place for formal prayer as a part of the liturgy of the church. But, for the moment, let us concentrate on a very personal type of talking with God in a family setting. Here there is no place for pretense. We are urged to go into the "closet." Here we can remove our masks and show our true faces. Conscious of acceptance by the Father (because of what Jesus has done for us), we can afford to expose our innermost thoughts and let the white light of truth explore our minds and hearts. This is no time for strutting and letting God know how nice we are. He knows better anyway. Remember the publican and the Pharisee?

Because our Father is faithful even above his promises, we can dare to admit we have failed, we can confess our sins—our specific sins. David and others were so forthright in their supplication that they dared to argue with God. This is the kind of honesty that gives us clues to the practical aspect of grace.

Indeed the pattern prayer which the Lord taught his disciples included petition for such down-to-earth things as groceries. Yet the same prayer deals with our repeated need for forgiveness, victory over temptation, and for power to live.

But the model prayer keeps us mindful that God is holy— his name is to be hallowed (venerated). He receives our worship, our adoration, our praise. We pray for the extension of his kingdom and for our submission to his will. Properly, all these elements of prayer precede our supplication, petition, and intercession.

Yet God, holy and exalted, does not stand on ceremony. Like the daughter of a President, we can dash into the Oval Office with freedom. "Let us then with confidence draw near to the throne of grace, that we may receive mercy and find grace to help in time of need" (Hebrews 4:16 RSV).

A new convert attending my wife's Bible class did not know about the proper forms of speaking to God, but she was willing to offer the opening prayer: "Good morning, dear Lord . . . ," she began. God heard that salutation in the high court of heaven!

Surely, prayers can be dull and routine. But we are expressly told that we are not heard for our "much speaking," to use King James English, or "vain repetition." How many dear brothers and sisters have failed to get that message!

One of the most soul-satisfying endeavors is intercession. That means praying for others. Our natural penchant is to be concerned about our own needs, our own frustrations, our own gripes. Intercessory prayer takes us out of ourselves and involves us with others. This is one of the most therapeutic means of dispelling depression and gnawing fears. Prayer is thus a major force in enabling us to grow up both spiritually and emotionally.

How sorry we are, wallowing in our own ugly self-centeredness. The very essence of maturity is a sense of personal responsibility and outward looking concern for others. We used to jokingly accuse our children of observing the maxim: "After me, others." This was said lightly to our children but alas, children do not have a monopoly on selfishness.

But many believers will tell you that they find it difficult to pray. Perhaps praying in public is not the way to start. Until we have learned to pour out our hearts in our own "closets" or the privacy of family devotions, we had better leave public prayer to those who have moved beyond the infant stage of self-consciousness.

But even though prayer seems to be our response to God, our Father, the two other members of the Trinity stand ready to help us—the Lord Jesus Christ himself who at the present time is in heaven appearing ". . . in the presence of God for us" (Hebrews 9:24), and the Holy Spirit within us. Both are described as intercessors on our behalf. Here is the classic Scripture passage that describes the work of the Spirit:

"In the same way the Spirit comes to the aid of our weakness. We do not even know how we ought to pray, but through our inarticulate groans the Spirit himself is pleading for us, and God who searches our inmost being knows what the Spirit means, because he pleads for God's people in God's own way" (Romans 8:26, 27 NEB).

We all feel guilty because we do not pray enough. Are we not told to "pray without ceasing?" But what can we do about it?

Since we are creatures of habit, it is important to follow a regimen of prayer. Ideally it is good to have a Q. T. (quiet time), as the British call it, when one regularly meets the Lord in prayer and devotional Bible reading. This might better be called a time for private worship, for in such a setting one comes into the presence of Christ who is revealed by the Scriptures. The time of day does not matter, but a regular time set aside for such prayer and worship can revolutionize the life of an aspiring Christian.

The Pauline epistles show us a man who was constantly interrupting his own train of thought to break forth into thanksgiving and praise. His doxologies have become a regular part of our public worship, even though they were probably first uttered as personal outbursts of praise.

No one can be goaded into building a prayer life for himself, but without prayer we will never progress in spiritual growth. To neglect prayer is to assure our continued spiritual infancy.

But the way of enrichment, joy and fulfilment is open to every believer.

May God grant this bountiful life to you!

14

Better Take the Guided Tour

Years ago an exuberant friend of mine announced that the Lord had guided him in the purchase of a used car. He was almost ecstatic in his declaration that God had led him to that wonderful buy.

Several weeks later I met my friend on the street and asked him about his new purchase.

Quite vehemently he responded. "Oh, that pile of junk. I got rid of it."

The Holy Spirit speaks with a soft voice. We ought to learn from his example. Our pious-sounding phrases and loud professions of faith may not be initiated by the Spirit. My friend's spiritual immaturity was showing. I am glad to report that he later grew in understanding and learned to speak with more restraint about God's leading.

This chapter might be regarded as an extension of the shorter one on prayer. Here we are dealing with the means of obtaining guidance from God. So many people are confused about knowing his will. At first glance this material may seem to be repetitive rehashing of principles already dealt with. Yet an attempt is made here to deal with all of the factors which can give the sincere believer surer means of obtaining divine guidance in specific situations. Admittedly we employ the same means of grace for both long- and short-range spiritual goals.

God has brought us into a warm, loving relationship with himself. Despite our sin and imperfection the Lord communicates his desires to us. The marvel of grace is that we are able to hear his voice and, in return, respond to him.

This life-in-relationship with the author of our new nature is the normative state of the believer, as we have indicated earlier. We depend on a God who communicates his will to us. It is not a dependence on an external code of laws or principles. Even the divinely-given Ten Commandments cannot save us or give us power to live a righteous life. The law of God only forces us back to dependence on a loving Savior.

"I know, O Lord, that the way of man is not in himself, that it is not in man who walks to direct his steps" (Jeremiah 10:23 RSV).

But just how do we get the message of guidance? Do we depend on common sense, gut feelings, or mystical experiences? Since we have been given good minds can we not simply reason things out?

No. It is in Holy Scripture that the Christian must find his basic spiritual and moral direction. However, our minds must be illuminated by the Holy Spirit, the divine interpreter of Scripture.

Nor can we circumvent the clear teaching of Scripture by saying that we have prayed about the matter and therefore have the guidance we need. Our voiced prayer is the human side of the transaction. It is a necessary means but not an end in itself. Besides, our hearts may subtly deceive us. Our prayers are too often cries of self-centered desire. We are easily led into thinking that God will give a favorable nod to prayers that reek of selfishness. God will give us what is best for us. That is why he frequently does not grant our requests.

For example, the Scriptures teach quite plainly that believers are not to be married to unbelievers (2 Corinthians 6:14). Yet how frequently a young person will insist that "I've prayed about it and I know that our marriage is God's will." No such rationalizing or wishful thinking can put the stamp of God's approval on disobedience.

Our hearts were distressed recently by the action of a talented minister who left his wife and children. Even though a gifted Bible teacher, he sought to rationalize his action by quoting Scriptures and giving "spiritual" explanations for his irresponsible act. This man's desertion of his wife and children was plainly opposed to God's will. How many lives have been wrecked because Christians seek to evade the teaching or deny the authority of Holy Scripture?

The seemingly arbitrary standards of Scripture, actually work for our good. God should not be envisioned as the one who forbids everything that is enjoyable. The "thou-shalt-not's" may be negative in their grammatical construction but they always work positively in our best interest as human beings. God is not a spoilsport. He is the personification of love.

When I put my little dog on a leash in the yard it is not to punish her but to protect her, so that she will not be killed by a passing car. Likewise the commandments of God are for our ultimate good.

It is impossible to know God's will for our guidance and growth if we are vague about the Word of God. It is a basic foundational aspect of Christian faith.

"All scripture is given by inspiration of God, and is profitable for doctrine, for reproof, for correction, for instruction in righteousness" (2 Timothy 3:16).

Christians who neglect the Bible totally miss its role in increasing our friendship with and love for Jesus Christ. The Scriptures are instrumental in initiating our union and maintaining our communion with him. But the Scriptures are not an end in themselves. As Jesus told his countrymen: "You search the scriptures, because you think that in them you have eternal life; and it is they that bear witness to me" (John 5:39 RSV).

We increasingly see the inter-relatedness of the various means of grace. We cannot separate the indwelling work of the Holy Spirit from the way in which Holy Scripture is opened to our hearts and minds. Thus "when he, the Spirit of truth is come, he will guide you into all truth" (John 16:13). Yet this does not happen apart from Scripture. Above all Christ himself is truth—not truth as an abstraction but truth that is embodied in a person.

There is another aspect of guidance which is as important as all that has gone before, namely, providence. By this we mean that God is ultimately in control of men and events. Often we seem to be facing a stone wall of impossibility. Yet God can transform circumstances which appear incapable of change. Truly he is the God of the impossible. The way in which God alters the course of human events as it suits his purpose can be seen in the story of Elijah, who prayed that there be no rain in Israel, and it did not rain for three and a half years (James 5:17).

The trusting Christian realizes that God is able to make a way where there is no way. When the Lord led the children of Israel out of Egypt to the edge of the Red Sea, what a predicament the Israelites were in: hemmed in by mountains, desert, and sea, they were pursued by the Egyptian chariots and horsemen. Yet it was at such a juncture that the Almighty delivered his people by leading them across the dry sea bed towards the Promised Land.

Perhaps you have dreaded a confrontation with a person who in the past has been hostile and unbending. After you have sought the Lord's guidance, however, the dreaded meeting turns out to be no problem. His entire attitude is different. All smiles, he greets you and his hostility has melted. "When a man's ways please the Lord, he makes even his enemies to be at peace with him" (Proverbs 16:7 RSV).

How can such things be explained except in the light of the providence of God?

Since the Christian is not simply an independent entity but is organically related to the community, it is in this corporate setting that individual believers are helped in seeking guidance. Pastors, elders, and the fathers of the Christian community can give counsel and guidelines. Particularly those who are young in the faith can receive help from more mature believers who have walked with the Lord for a longer period of time.

Most of us try to understand and solve our problems on our own. But we are dismayed when we find that we are faced with so many gray areas. We cannot determine what is black and what is white. That is when the counsel of those gifted by God is invaluable.

"Obey your leaders and defer to them; for they are tireless in their concern for you . . ." (Hebrews 13:17 NEB).

Furthermore, in the body of Christ all believers are to be in submission to one another. If we accept this spirit of life together, we can be surer of obtaining the divine guidance we seek.

But there are still other means for getting directions from God. In the long course of redemptive history, God has given certain individuals guidance through messages delivered by angels. The New Testament does not give us much light on the role of angels today, but somehow they silently serve us. "Are [angels] not all ministering spirits, sent forth to minister for them who shall be heirs of salvation?" (Hebrews 1:14).

God also sometimes speaks to us through dreams and visions. Today many Christians in the charismatic renewal depend greatly on the gift of prophetic utterance as guidance both for individuals and for the community. Certainly prophetic utterance, that is, a direct revelation from God for a specific situation, was frequently heard in the infant church. Today, this is a controversial subject and I for one feel that the gift of prophecy may be misused, as may any of the gifts of the Spirit. But events in my own experience prevent me from being quick to rule out any of the gifts of the Spirit for today.

But all extraordinary means of guidance—and here I should place angels, visions, dreams, and prophetic utterance—have limitations set upon them. Our objective external authority is the Word of God. Some hint of this is given by the Apostle Paul himself:

"But though we, or an angel from heaven, preach any other gospel unto you than that which we have preached unto you, let him be accursed" (Galatians 1:8).

The chief human means of seeking guidance is simple: *We ask for it.* This means praying where specific guidance is sought, not only for general wisdom.

The place of prayer in the lives of the patriarchs, the prophets, and the great saints of both Old and New Testaments certainly is known to all. The prayers of David and Daniel are particularly important in our spiritual heritage, and access to the very throne of God is one of the marks of the new age. We are urged to approach the throne boldly.

Let us recall the benevolent invitation of Jesus Christ, our Lord:

"Ask, and it shall be given you; seek, and ye shall find; knock, and it shall be opened unto you" (Luke 11:9).

As prayer becomes a habit of our lives, we develop greater confidence that we will be rightly led by God. Then as we know his will, and do it, we learn the joy of continuing fellowship with him and obedience is easier.

How do we know we are on course? Knowing the will of

God and seeking the Lord's guidance do not fit into a simplistic formula. Because of what we are and because of the world in which we live, it is often difficult to determine the will of God.

If we would know the will of God, first we must follow the injunction of Romans 12:1, 2 that we offer our bodies as living sacrifices to God so that we may experience the renewal of our minds that we "may prove what is that good, and acceptable, and perfect, will of God." Romans 6 indicates that we must make yielding ourselves to God a daily life pattern.

How often we flounder helplessly about when we have not taken the first step of a spirit yielded to God.

We tend to forget the presence of God within us in the person of the indwelling Holy Spirit. You may ask how we can distinguish between the guidance of the Holy Spirit and the inward promptings of our own human spirit? Just how can we be certain that we are being directed by the Holy Spirit? Don't forget my friend who bought the car and the preacher who left his wife.

The question demands a serious reply. Probably the most important check on subjectivism is in the objective revelation of Holy Scripture. The Holy Spirit is not capricious. He always operates in harmony with the teaching of the Bible. It is inconceivable that the Holy Spirit would lead anyone in a direction contrary to scriptural principles.

But you say, "I can't always understand the Bible. It's a difficult book." Well, there is much truth to that. But stop a minute. The Bible contains the Ten Commandments, which are stated in easily comprehensible terms. Does your "guidance" in any way contravene the holy commandments? If so, try again!

There are other tests, too. Examine your own motivation. Does your "guidance" exalt you rather than Jesus Christ? Does your "guidance" benefit your family, friends or neighbors? Is your "guidance" motivated by love? Is your "guidance" consistent with what has been the continuing will of God in your life?

The indwelling Holy Spirit, if you are honest and let him, will certainly show you the truth, and guide you in the right direction for you.

As this spiritual exercise becomes a part of you—for our faith and understanding can grow—you will find it is easier to know what is the proper course for you.

15

Both Word and Deed

"What is spirituality? A worn Bible and a frown for mini-skirts? Attendance at Wednesday evening prayer meetings and Walt Disney movies only? Supernatural without natural, soul without body, sacred without secular? How can I be *me*, without part of *me* being shrunk to the size of a skeleton-in-the-closet Christian? Without my life losing the full dimension, God wants it to have in the Spirit?"[1]

These are questions posed in a magazine article by Harvie M. Conn, noted author and student of the history of missions. Conn strikes a note that is missing from so many volumes dealing with spiritual growth. It is a sad fact that there is a tendency for most books on Christian piety to concentrate on one's *inner life*, one's dramatic *personal* experience, one's concern for *internal* holiness. While it may be true that moral and spiritual issues are centered in the heart, there is great peril in becoming too introspective, too concerned about ourselves, too other-worldly.

Such concerns for holiness have driven well-motivated people away from a world populated by people in need.

1. Harvie M. Conn, "Can I Be Spiritual and at the Same Time Human?" *The Other Side*, Sept.–Oct., 1973.

Admittedly there is a place for a "desert experience" for a limited time as in the case of both Moses and Paul, but they certainly did not remain isolated. Their desert discipline prepared them for active service in behalf of the people of God.

Certainly we are to be concerned about our own Christian growth but not apart from taking up the towel in lowly service. The love which is generated in our hearts by the Holy Spirit does not exist apart from action nor apart from an object.

The example held up before us throughout the Word and in the Sacraments is that God so loved the world of people that he did something about it. In his love he experienced more than a warm emotion or a good feeling in his heart. He sent his Son to die for us. The goal of love is reached by painful, sacrificial action. So our love must show forth in our lives if we are to grow up into Christ.

During his earthly ministry our Lord demonstrated his love by a life of intense activity. He shared in the lives of people, ministering to them through healings of the heart and mind and soul. He spoke to them in those unforgettable words on the Mount, but his was always more than a verbal ministry. He had compassion for people; he did something about their physical and spiritual needs. There was no dichotomy between spiritual and physical. All was *spiritual* ministry whether for the body or soul. He was concerned for the whole being of those he loved and served.

Thus Jesus is our exemplar for what it means to be a mature person. He preached the gospel of the Kingdom, the new era and rule that he inaugurated. In its full glory the Kingdom was yet to come, but he also demonstrated how Kingdom people were to live and grow and serve here and now.

Earlier we have noted that the goal of Christian growth is ultimate conformity to the image of the Son of God. We are to live with growing evidence of our likeness to Christ by *living out* the principles of the Kingdom. That means a life of divinely energized, loving activity. It is not mere activism—frenetic action without the Spirit's constant direction. (There is no merit in action for its own sake.) Love in the biblical sense flows from Spirit-filled people and results in all manner of good works in behalf of other people—our neighbors, and especially those in the household of faith.

That love is not abstract or only expressed verbally is clearly explained: "By this we know love, that he laid down his life for us; and we ought to lay down our lives for the brethren. But if any one has the world's goods and sees his brother in need, yet closes his heart against him, how does God's love abide in him? Little children, let us not love in word or speech but in deed and in truth" (1 John 3:16–18 RSV).

The full blaze of the Kingdom's glory has not yet filled the new heavens and new earth. Yet those of us whom God has delivered from the dominion of darkness and transferred to the Kingdom of his beloved Son (Colossians 1:13) should be occupied to some degree in establishing "kingdom enclaves" insofar as we are able. While we have no illusions about complete renovation of the present evil world, we should be concerned about its evils and stand against them. We minister to people where we find them. To what degree the maturing Christian should involve himself in social concern and action is not spelled out in Scripture. But we are to be "zealous of good works." The Holy Spirit will guide each of us, some one way, some another.

Conservative Christians have rightly insisted upon preaching the gospel. I believe that there is indeed a primacy about declaring the *message* of the gospel. I find myself increasingly disturbed by those who stretch the meaning of the word "gospel" to include "social action."

Yet the Scriptures indicate that it is as important for a Christian *to do good* as it is to preach the gospel. Christians have not been placed in the world as passive onlookers, only waiting for Christ to return (as he surely will), but as active witnesses. We are not navel gazers, concerned only about our own spiritual growth. We are to be involved in the lives of those about us.

". . . Let us not be weary in well doing . . . As we have therefore opportunity, let us do good unto all men, especially unto them who are of the household of faith" (Galatians 6:9-10).

In the same context of Scripture, we are enjoined: "Bear ye one another's burdens, and so fulfil the law of Christ" (Galatians 6:2).

There should be no breach in the Body of Christ over the relative importance of preaching the gospel and engaging in good works. What spiritual myopia to divorce from each other these essential mandates of our risen Lord! If we are to be growing Christians we must not live "unto ourselves" but be involved both by word and deed in the lives of others.

I am uncomfortable with people who leave a tract and a small tip for the waitress in a restaurant. While I believe that printed material can be profitably used in the communication of the gospel, giving a tract can never substitute for giving ourselves. Even our Lord felt that virtue had gone out of him when the hem of his garment was touched by a woman seeking healing; so we also will find that it costs in time and effort to minister to the wounded in heart and mind. That is why we are called "laborers."

Perhaps conservative Christians of this era have concentrated so much on our obtaining salvation by grace alone that we are inclined to stop there. Most certainly it is grace and not our own meager efforts that draw us to God. But once we experience his salvation we possess his power for an active life of good works.

"For you were called to freedom, brethren," the Apostle Paul tells the Galatians; "only do not use your freedom as an opportunity for the flesh, but through love be servants of one another" (Galatians 5:13 RSV).

In the grand plan of God "we are his workmanship, created in Christ Jesus for good works, which God prepared beforehand, that we should walk in them" (Ephesians 2:10 RSV).

Harvie Conn feels there are two definitions of spirituality prevalent in the world today: what he dubs "world-centered" spirituality which emphasizes ministry to bodies rather than souls, and "soul-centered" spirituality. The former, he says, reshapes spiritual service into a framework as large as the world, the other into one "as small as a man's vest pocket prayer list."[2]

Conn warns that world-centered spirituality wipes out the lines separating "church" and "world." It concentrates on the here and now, ultimately involving the church in political-social revolution.

But Conn feels that soul-centered spirituality by itself is as wrong as the "world-centered" variety. This emphasis, which characterizes so much literature on personal holiness and piety, is dangerous in that it is exclusively other-worldly.

The maturing Christian needs to avoid these one-dimensional concepts of spirituality. It is encouraging that evangelicals, especially since the Lausanne Conference of 1974, have returned to their earlier concern for social justice. Perhaps this stems from a realization that Christ's redemptive plan includes not only making new creatures but also establishing a new order. This order will not come into being by human effort. But the Kingdom is both present and future, and the same One who will dramatically create the

2. Harvie M. Conn, "Can I Be Spiritual and at the Same Time Human?" *The Other Side*, Sept.–Oct., 1973.

new heavens and new earth is now working in and *through* his people.

The reduction of Christian spirituality to a narrow concern for one's own personal growth and future state is an error which comes from an identification of "the spiritual with the non-physical" which, says Conn, "is completely unintelligible by New Testament standards." Instead the epistles are "filled with discussions of the 'spiritual life' that cover topics like political exploitation, social intolerance, the consumption of foods used in pagan ceremonies, the position of women, family relationships, the propriety of dress, relationships with non-Christians, taxation, prostitution, homosexuality, the relief of poverty."[3]

Perceptively, Conn does not advocate employing "carnal" weapons for spiritual warfare. Instead he shows that "the warlord of the universe" did not enter Jerusalem on a charger but a donkey. And "He gives to his people for rule, not a scepter, but a towel." Our weapons against all sorts of social injustice are the "fruit" of the Spirit.

While we are about the task of preaching the gospel and performing good works, let us be concerned about the emotional climate in which we operate. We should radiate joy, not grimness, if we would effectively communicate the good news.

When I was a university student, I attended a Bible class conducted by a physician who sacrificially devoted his life to the company of Christians in which I was reared. He had a stern appearance and most of the "saints" lived in mortal fear of him.

I learned a lot about the Bible from this man. He had a good grasp of Christian truth and he was a capable teacher. Yet I do not recall his ever spending much time on Christian joy. Instead, he often stressed the fact that our Lord was a

3. Harvie M. Conn, "Can I Be Spiritual and at the Same Time Human?" *The Other Side*, Sept.–Oct., 1973.

Man of Sorrows, who was acquainted with grief. He taught that Christians should be sober and avoid frivolity. He and his tight-lipped wife were the living embodiment of his teaching.

I am more than a little troubled by the large percentage of Christian people who seem to have no joy. The really "spiritual" ones always seem so tense. Dare I say that they seem to place such an emphasis upon their personal holiness that one is uncomfortable in their presence? In fact, I have often felt more comfortable with my unregenerate friends because they were more aware of their sinnerhood, or so it seemed. Would that the "saints" were more aware of *their* sinfulness.

I would like to argue for a quality of Christian living that shows more tolerance and acceptance of people of diverse personalities and backgrounds without in any way intimating an acceptance of sin. The Christians who have most influenced me are those who were brimful of love and good spirits. They were secure enough in their faith to have a sense of humor—to realize in a deep down practical way that nothing is so authentic or contagious as Christian joy.

Most of us would reveal our growing maturity if we took ourselves a little less seriously. I think there is ample evidence in Scripture that God has a sense of humor.

Could anything be funnier than the story of Gideon in the book of Judges? Perhaps you think of Gideon as the hero who rescued Israel from the marauding Midianites. For these victories Gideon was made a judge of Israel and in Hebrews 11 he is listed as one of the great heroes of the faith.

But if you examine the text of Judges carefully you will find that Gideon is about the last person you would pick as a potential hero. Actually, he was a coward. When he appears on the scene, he is hiding in the hills, threshing wheat in the shadow of a big winepress. That is where he is found by the angel of the Lord, who hails the unlikely hero with these words: "The Lord is with thee, thou mighty man of valor" (Judges 6:12).

Every time I read that passage I laugh again. Some hero! Gideon continually finds fault with God's dealing with Israel. He demonstrates neither valor not great faith.

The Lord must have a sense of humor to call Gideon "a man of valor." But in this amusing situation God's abounding grace is demonstrated. Who else can make a hero out of a clod! What a cosmic joke that God can take hunks of clay and make saints out of them. It makes me roar with laughter until I weep for joy.

G. K. Chesterton used to say; "The reason why I am a Christian is because it is such fun." If we recognize what God had done for us through Christ's suffering and sorrow, we are humbled before him and we can see ourselves in truer perspective. We can then appropriately recall Jesus' words in the parable of the talents, "Enter thou into the joy of the Lord" (Matthew 25:21).

The Christian life is not a burdensome joyless pilgrimage. It is exciting to be caught up in the purposes of God and to be involved in the lives of people. One of the biggest falsehoods promulgated by Satan is that following Jesus makes for a drab life. There is no place for being "sad, sullen or strained," as someone has put it.

Think back on the unrestrained joy that marked the homecoming party staged by the father for the Prodigal Son. They made merry with feasting and dancing. Or recall the wedding party at Cana that was made even merrier by our Lord's first miracle. There is "a time to weep, and a time to laugh," says the Preacher (Ecclesiastes 3:4).

The uptight zealot, overly concerned with his "testimony," may be far less spiritually mature than the believer who has learned to relax and rest in the joyful promises of God.

Which brings up another point: the place of work and the

need for rest. Work is important. It is often therapeutic for our disoriented lives. But let us remember that the Bible also teaches the need for rest and recreation.

The Lord Jesus explained that the sabbath was made for man and not man for the sabbath. The sabbatarian principle of six days of work and one day of rest is a divinely ordained rhythm of life. We ignore this to our own peril. The Pharisees changed God's law into an intolerable legalistic burden. That is why they were so distressed when the Lord healed the man on the sabbath. They acted like a policeman zealously giving out tickets for over-parking while the murderer escapes.

It was the Lord himself who saw the plight of his disciples who were so busy with the "many coming and going" that they did not have time to eat. The Lord urged them to get away from the grind and take a few days of rest in the desert sunshine (Mark 6:31). He was not fearful that the cosmic clock of redemption would stop if the workers took some time off.

Perhaps we need to be more concerned about humility as we serve others. The attitude that exalts machismo—that ideal of the unliberated male—probably regards humility and meekness as softness and spinelessness. But it was the Lord of heaven who demonstrated that it is in seeming weakness that we can be the strongest. Jesus was able to humble himself and accept death on the cross. He "did not count equality with God a thing to be grasped, but emptied himself, taking the form of a servant . . ."(Philippians 2:6-7 RSV).

Likewise we can take on lowly tasks because he has made us "kings and priests unto God" (Revelation 1:6). No menial work can take away the consciousness of our value to God.

It is the insecure, immature man who struts and clamors for acclaim. The believer who knows he is redeemed by the blood of Christ and made a partaker of the divine nature does not have to prove himself. This is the pilgrim who is learning to serve without fanfare, abandoning the childish need for public attention.

There are so many rewarding ways of serving. Just giving money to the Lord is one of them. I have never known a Christian who had made progress in the life of faith who has not learned to give.

"Give, and it will be given to you; good measure, pressed down, shaken together, running over, will be put into your lap. For the measure you give will be the measure you get back" (Luke 6:38 RSV).

To share our possessions with the needy enriches life in a way that no other discipline can. We live in a materialistic society of conspicuous consumption. The prevailing sin of our day is covetousness and greed, which the Bible classifies as idolatry. Our Lord was always concerned with the poor. Of course there are "welfare chiselers," but let us not belabor that subject. We could be seeking a scapegoat for our own lack of compassion.

Giving is a God-like quality, and as we begin to emulate his practice we will experience revolutionary changes within our own being.

One form of giving, almost dying out in our secularized world, is the ministry of hospitality. To open our homes to entertain strangers will bring rewards in the quality of our lives. It takes planning and expense to serve a meal in these days of escalating expense. Besides the logistics and burden of shopping at the supermarket, planning the menu, preparing the vegetables, washing the lettuce and making the salad, cooking, serving and—anticlimax of anticlimaxes— washing the dishes and the table linens is work, usually for the overburdened woman.

But what rich rewards there are in getting to know one's friends in a deeper way, and this is the ideal setting for

Christian fellowship. Then, too, hospitality may be a low-key step toward sharing our faith effectively.

When you put yourself out to provide a dinner, you compliment your guests by this very act. You show them that you care enough about them to give something of yourself. Yet you gain the most, for it is still more blessed to give than to receive.

In these and other practical expressions, Christians have countless opportunities to demonstrate the measure of the abundant life they enjoy. In such ways we not only grow in likeness to Christ, but we also expand the horizons of the new realm in which we live. We can exalt Christ in the most mundane areas of life.

Our Lord himself set the example when he prepared breakfast for his disciples on the shore of the lake in one of his post-resurrection appearances. Earlier he had turned water into wine and dismay into rejoicing at the wedding in Cana. One day in the future he will act as host at the marriage supper of the Lamb.

16

Exhortation and Doxology

St. Augustine stands out in the long line of the great Fathers
of the church. He was a great sinner and a great saint who
came to know the healing grace of Christ. With a clear vision
of the City of God, his feet were planted on the earth, where
he learned to walk as a servant and a seer. He knew the
importance of a balanced life of devotion and service. Hear
him:

"No man has a right to lead such a life of contemplation as
to forget in his own ease the service due to his neighbor; nor
has any man a right to be so immersed in active life as to
neglect the contemplation of God."

This quotation catches some of what I hoped to present in
this little book. I have also sought to arouse the multitudes
of quiescent brothers and sisters within the church who
float with the stream and devote themselves to what the
late Abraham Maslow, the psychologist, calls "evasion of
growth." Our churches are filled with gifted Christians. Yet
only a relatively small percentage of this vast army have
discovered the dynamism within them which in an earlier
day "turned the world upside down."

The late Watchman Nee, who wrote so effectively on this
condition, has these observations which I must pass along:

"Spiritual wealth comes not from special gifts of grace on special occasions, but from unremitting divine activity in a human life over years of time. It is a grief to me to find brothers and sisters so dependent on special experiences that, between the periodic help these bring, they lapse into a life indistinguishable from that of the pagans around them. What a poverty-striken state this reveals! They are laying in store no riches. Between the temporary lift they get from Christian meetings or other means of grace, they lived a life of defeat. The life of the Spirit is not like that. Its wealth is not gained at the halting-places of life, but through the ceaseless operation of God's grace on the long stretch of the road between."[1]

As I immersed myself in research, I became increasingly aware that Christian growth cannot be gained by a simplistic formula. It is striking that so many of the great books on holiness and related themes seem to stress one aspect of truth, such as the ministry of the Holy Spirit or the place of the Word of God in fostering spirituality. I have sought to avoid harping on a single theme.

In this book I have tried to give some idea of the multi-faceted aspects of the means of growth, yet I am sure that much more can be said. For example, I have not mentioned explicitly the many models who have had an impact on my own life. Some of them were gifted public figures like Paul Tournier and Helmut Thielicke. Some, like Donald Grey Barnhouse, Stacey Woods, John Stott, Northcote Deck and several others, were associates in some aspect of Christian endeavor. Most of all I am indebted to the loving influence of my late father, Lewis L. Hitt, who was my boyhood example of commitment to Jesus Christ.

Beyond those I have known personally are the authors of

---

1. Watchman Nee, *A Table in the Wilderness*, Fort Washington, Pa.: Christian Literature Crusade, 1966.

books that have been a major source of awakening latent sensibilities and widening a vision of the good life.

Finally, we have not begun to tap the fountainhead of truth in Holy Scripture. The latter portions of the New Testament epistles stress the practical aspects of day-to-day living. The "strong man" of Romans 14 is responsible enough to be concerned for the weaker brother. There are many more examples. But I must not rob you of the fun of discovery.

May "the God of peace . . . make you perfect in every good work to do his will, working in you that which is wellpleasing in his sight, through Jesus Christ . . ." (Hebrews 13:20, 21).

Additional Reading

These are the books I have found helpful and I would recommend to those who wish to do further reading. I should list nearly all the works of Helmut Thielicke, Paul Tournier, C. S. Lewis, and John R. W. Stott, rector emeritus of All Souls' Church, London.

Donald G. Bloesch, *The Crisis of Piety*, Grand Rapids: Eerdmans, 1968.

Dietrich Bonhoeffer, *The Cost of Discipleship*, London: Student Christian Movement, 1948.

Hugh Evan Hopkins, *The Mystery of Suffering*, Downers Grove, Ill.: Inter-Varsity Press, 1959.

Ronald Knox, *Enthusiasm*, Oxford: Clarendon Press, 1950.

K. F. W. Prior, *The Way of Holiness*, Downers Grove, Ill.: Inter-Varsity Press, 1967.

Lewis B. Smedes, *All Things Made New*, Grand Rapids: Eerdmans, 1970.

James I. Packer, *Knowing God*, Downers Grove, Ill.: Inter-Varsity Press, 1975.

Jordan Aumann, Thomas Hopko, and Donald G. Bloesch, *Christian Spirituality East and West*, Chicago, Ill.: Priory Press, 1968.

Ralph Martin, *Hungry for God*, Old Tappan, N.J.: Spire, 1976.

John Powell, S. J., *He Touched Me*, Niles, Ill.: Argus Communications, 1974.

Watchman, Nee, *The Normal Christian Life*, Fort Washington, Pa.: Christian Literature Crusade, 1963.

Other Approaches to Holiness

Throughout the history of the church, there have been many varieties of emphasis on the best way to live the Christian life—communal, institutional, monastic—and many efforts, since the Reformation, to regain the purity and vitality that presumably existed in the infant church.

It is true that some of the emphases of past generations degenerated into heresy and a departure from historic, biblically-derived faith. At other times the pendulum has swung toward warmth and vitality, as in the Great Awakening of our own colonial history.

But in all periods including the Middle Ages there were bright spots. There are many models of devotion to Christ and selfless service in the monastic and ascetic tradition. Likewise there were extravagant excesses of enthusiasm in the greatest of the revivals.

Most of us are unacquainted with the ebb and flow of religious history. Whether it is because of spiritual illiteracy on our part or because certain sinister forces persistently oppose the Kingdom of God, ancient error and wrong emphases have always dogged the path of the Christian faith.

A quick rundown of a few of the trends of history may give

us better balance in maintaining biblical and apostolic verities and rejecting errors. These reflections are highly selective and personal.

Activism—I once knew an evangelist who conceived that his great mission in life was to acquaint as many people with the claims of Christ as he could possibly reach in his life span. The primary means he employed was the distribution of gospel tracts. I am sure that within the ten years or more our lives touched, this strongly motivated Christian disposed of tons of religious literature. Yet neither he nor I would have any idea of how effective his method was in bringing men and women to the knowledge of God.

I painfully recall an occasion when he was riding with me in my car. The window on his side of the vehicle was open. As we rode along, he was tossing tracts out the window, solemnly declaring, "We must always be sowing the seed."

Through my rearview mirror I could see the tracts flying through the air, landing in the receding fields and puddles of water. It struck me that I was witnessing an example of misguided zeal. My friend was a devout Christian, but as I review his conduct I think he equated activity with effective witness.

This may be a far-fetched example of what I believe is a trend in American Christian religious work. We seem to confuse frenetic activity with being faithful to Jesus Christ. Ours is not a meditative culture. We pride ourselves on action, whether our theology is conservative or liberal. Evangelicals concentrate on mammoth campaigns that sometimes turn out to be ineffective for the long pull.

Social activists are so busy inventing new ways to improve the world that they forget they are dealing with human beings desperately in need of the healing, saving touch of Jesus Christ. There is greater interest in solving social, political, and economic problems than in providing spiritually starved people with the bread of life.

The essential problem with activism is lack of perspective. Certainly Christians must always be involved in creative forms of evangelism and concerned about the social problems which plague our world. But activism too often means an emphasis on evangelism at the expense of good works. Or vice versa.

Evangelical activism also tends to stress methodology at the expense of theological integrity and balance. There are all sorts of programs in the religious world that offer us pre-packaged spiritual kits or quick shortcuts to holiness. Such assembly line methods of developing our spiritual life are particularly odious to me.

Our Lord's life was full of activity. Yet he had time for individuals and he was marked by compassion. Perhaps the true antidote to activism may be found in his practice of maintaining close union with his Father. To sustain this relationship, he spent hours in prayer and meditation.

Asceticism—At the very outset of a look at asceticism or ascetic theology, we run into semantic difficulties. There is a wide difference between the Catholic tradition which makes spirituality and asceticism virtual synonyms for Christian growth, and the evangelical tradition which regards ascetic practices with caution or disapproval.

Protestants possess a very limited literature on spirituality. They tend to eschew the terms "spirituality" and "asceticism" since both evoke images of what are regarded as "medieval" practices, such as penance, celibacy, and various extreme forms of self-denial. Evangelicals generally employ the words piety or sanctification when dealing with the concept of Christian growth.

In recent years scholars have been conducting ecumenical seminars in which the Roman Catholic, the Eastern Orthodox, and evangelical positions on spirituality have been explored. Such consultations have opened doors of understanding which should benefit the whole church.

Protestants as well as Catholics have long profited from the *Confessions* of St. Augustine and *The Imitation of Christ* by Thomas à Kempis. For many years evangelicals concerned with piety have read *The Practice of the Presence of God* by Brother Lawrence, a lay brother of the Carmelite order who served the Lord at humble kitchen tasks although by nature he despised them. The hymn books of Protestantism contain the poetry of many of pre-Reformation saints, none more beloved than Bernard of Clairvaux's "O Sacred Head."

But not many Protestants have read the works of St. John of the Cross and St. Theresa of Avila. Both of these Catholic saints were exponents of "rigorous asceticism, mystical devotion, and the contemplative life."[1] Of aristocratic birth, St. Theresa and St. John might be regarded as elitist in their strategy of reforming the church by spiritual renewal of the clergy.

John of the Cross was a student of the Arabian mystics and was well trained in Thomistic philosophy. Out of his personal experience he wrote three poems that trace the process of attaining intimate union with God: *The Ascent of Mount Carmel, Dark Night of the Soul,* and *Living Flame of Love.* The *Ascent* describes the preparatory steps of mortification, but this is followed by *Dark Night* in which the grace of God develops the positive side of growth. John recognizes that God, not man, accomplishes the real work of sanctification.

In the third work, the *Living Flame of Love,* St. John reaches concepts of perfection far above ordinary human experience. This is often described as the beatific vision, a state of perfect happiness in which God is seen face to face. In describing this experience, St. John employs terms of "oriental exuberance," yet the end result is not only joyous love for God but also for one's neighbor.

1. Sydney E. Ahlstrom, *A Religious History of the American People,* New Haven: Yale University Press, 1972.

St. Theresa also dealt with the development of the spiritual life in three major works: the *Life*, *The Way of Perfection*, and *The Interior Castle*. Later she wrote *Foundations*, an account of her convents. She developed a schema of the grades of prayer from meditation to the prayer of the transforming union. Yet she stated explicitly that "the highest perfection does not consist in interior consolations, sublime raptures, visions, or the gift of prophecy, but in the conformity of our will with God's, so that whatever we know he wants, we also desire with all our will; and we accept with as much joy that which is bitter as that which is sweet, knowing that it is his will."[2]

Even fewer Protestants have read the writings of St. Ignatius Loyola, founder of the Society of Jesus. First intent on a military career, he was injured in battle by a cannonball that mangled one leg. While recuperating he happened to read Ludolph of Saxony's *Life of Christ*. That inspired him to become a soldier for Christ. Later he built his Jesuit order on a paramilitary structure which stressed obedience, discipline, and efficiency. But before that he had entered a monastery and spent a year in ascetic discipline, experienced several visions and then written his manual on spiritual warfare and conquest, the *Spiritual Exercises*. In this enormously influential work, he devised a regimen for converting the soul from selfishness and worldliness to complete obedience to God's will.

There are strains of asceticism in Puritanism and German pietism. Some scholars feel that the latter movement was a revival of medieval monasticism and asceticism. Pietism's contribution to the Christian cause was a needed emphasis on holy living, Bible study, and missionary concern.

Self-denial per se cannot be faulted. Our Lord himself was a homeless itinerant who did not marry. He made strange

2. Theresa of Avila, *Foundations*.

statements such as that of Luke 14:26, 27: "If any man come to me, and hate not his father, and mother, and wife, and children, and brethren, and sisters, yea, and his own life also, he cannot be my disciple. And whosoever doth not bear his cross, and come after me, cannot be my disciple."

Such self-denial might include celibacy but as a "gift" from God neither pridefully self-willed nor imposed by external authority. Again he indicated that "those who are considered worthy of taking part in . . . the resurrection from the dead will neither marry nor be given in marriage, and they can no longer die; for they are like the angels" (Luke 20:35, 36 NIV). While this is sometimes taken as a basis for living an ascetic life here and now, the context indicates that Jesus was explaining that life in heaven would not be a mere prolongation of the earthly life as the Jews envisioned, but would be radically different.

The Apostle Paul advocated voluntary celibacy in 1 Corinthians 7, but a closer reading of the passage reveals that he felt marriage was the normal state for most believers. Only those to whom God gives the charism (gift) of celibacy should remain unmarried. He recognizes that the unmarried can more effectively serve the Lord, but each individual must order his life in the will of God.

Some asceticism developed from disgust with the material world, including the body. This sometimes led to all sorts of bizarre beliefs and practices of desert anchorites who sought to mortify their bodies by living separated, solitary lives. One such declared, "I am killing the body because it is killing me." It was out of ascetic impulses that monasticism developed.

Clement of Alexandria sought purification from passions as a condition of ascent to God. Origen, one of the revered Fathers of the church, took Matthew 19:12 literally and castrated himself. Admittedly this is an extreme case, for there is much in the ascetic tradition from which the entire church can benefit.

Even though the believer may for a time need the rigorous experience of desert training, his ministry is to the world. Denying self, he must live in the world even though he must always resist its deleterious influence. Holiness and growth and service are for all the people of God.

Origen's misplaced zeal highlights the peril of regarding the body rather than the "flesh" as the seat of our sinful urges. The Bible teaches us to mortify the deeds of the flesh but to cherish our bodies as temples of the Holy Spirit.

Without disparaging the great achievements of ascetic individuals and communities, one must recognize that there was often confusion about the place of meritorious works in achieving, or helping to obtain, salvation. The Reformation revived the primary place of free grace. How important to rest in the finished work of Christ!

Communalism—It has often been said that true communism was not initiated by Karl Marx but by the early Christians who had all things in common. This early Christian communism or communalism did not survive long in its purest form. Yet religious history is replete with the stories of groups seeking to recapture the spirit and life style of the first Christian community in Jerusalem.

No doubt monasticism was one effort to establish a "pure" Christian society that would escape the pollution of the world. In more recent history America has been the spawning ground for a number of colorful cooperative communities: the Bethel and Aurora communes of Missouri and Oregon, the Bishop Hill Commune of Illinois, Brook Farm and the Hopedale Community in Massachusetts, the Oneida Community in New York, and many others. No matter how bravely and expectantly the communities began, sooner or later they ended in failure.

Probably the "brotherhood" of the Anabaptists, in modern times, the Mennonites and Amish, has maintained the sense of a Christian community more than any other group. There is much the rest of the church can learn from the life style of these believers. When a barn burns down, for example, the Amish community joins together to help the brother who has suffered loss. Simplicity of life, thrift, honest toil, and strong familial ties are admirable aspects of the best in the Anabaptist tradition.

When the Jesus People rescued from evil influences certain aspects of the youth culture, they renewed the concept of Christian communal living. Later, the neo-Pentecostal movement embraced similar patterns in some instances. House churches, both charismatic and non-charismatic, have sprung up all over the country. In Ann Arbor, Michigan, the large Word of God Community, made up of charismatic Catholics and Protestants, has demonstrated a new ecumenism, a breaking down of denominational ties. Not all house churches can properly be described as cooperative communities but the communal spirit prevails.

The great peril of communalism is that of withdrawing from the world and escaping the burdens of the larger society. The commune or community becomes a strange hybrid, since it is neither the church nor the world, as the Bible seems to distinguish them. There is an inherent tendency for communities to become ingrown and to neglect the primary responsibility of evangelistic outreach and social concern. Instead, the upbuilding of the community and its members becomes of paramount concern. Even though there is much talk of breaking down sectarian barriers, when one refers to a "brother" he usually means a male member of the community, seldom a Christian in the church at large.

The divinely ordained community is the Body of Christ. With all its imperfections, we must find our Christian fellowship there and live within the household of faith, as delineated in Scripture.

Experientialism—The late Ronald Knox has given the church a great book *Enthusiasm,* which thoroughly documents the dangers of experientialism as a religious norm. By this term we mean that our religious "feelings" transcend the authority of both the Holy Spirit and Holy Scripture. It is not what we learn from the inspired and objective revelation of Scripture but what we discern subjectively that governs our Christian conduct.

Father Knox, who spent thirty years compiling his history of "enthusiasm," was tempted to call his work "ultrasupernaturalism," for, he said, "this is the real character of the enthusiast; he expects more evident results from the grace of God than we others. . . . He will have no 'almost-Christians,' no weaker brethren who plod and stumble. . . ."[3]

It is true that the Christian is involved in more than adhering to abstract doctrine and involving himself in certain ritual. We do experience love and joy and all the pleasures of the new life. But we must avoid making *our* experience the standard for others. (Think of Paul's visit to the third heaven!) Beyond that, our own experience varies with our emotions; we must not ever substitute it for the authoritative Word of God.

One of the controversial phenomena of our day is prophetic utterance, which comes from divine revelation applied to a specific contemporary situation. Without ruling out the possibility of the gift of prophecy for today, it must be evident to all that such spontaneous communication can be abused. Indeed the Bible warns us against false prophets. If such prophecies do arise, they must be tested by "the more sure word of prophecy," the Holy Scriptures.

Legalism—This widespread tendency in the church is always marked by the imposition of a code of extra-biblical structures to govern Christian behavior. The principal treatise in Scripture denouncing legalism is Paul's letter to the Galatians. This is an eloquent argument in behalf of the free grace of God. ". . . We know," says Paul, "that no man is

3. Ronald A. Knox, *Enthusiasm*, Oxford: Clarendon Press, 1950.

ever justified by doing what the law demands, but only through faith in Christ Jesus" (Galatians 2:15 NEB). The particular problem Paul faced was the demand by Peter and other leaders in the Jerusalem church that Gentile converts submit to circumcision. Paul declares that the new way of life means direction from the Spirit of God indwelling every believer. Thus if we walk in the Spirit, that is, are guided by him, we will not fall victim to the wanton desires of our human nature. "If the Spirit is the source of our life, let the Spirit also direct our course" (Galatians 5:25 NEB).

The Judaism of the Pharisees of Jesus' day had degenerated into a complex code that attempted to legislate the minutest aspects of human behavior. It was a load no human being could bear.

This same tendency to develop codes of conduct that go beyond Scripture has often been taken up by Christians with a zeal equal to that of the Pharisees. Legalism crops up constantly in every area of the church. We must be as watchful as Paul and not let it develop.

There is an interesting phrase in Deuteronomy 5:22 that follows the giving of the Ten Commandments: "These words the Lord spake unto all your assembly in the mount out of the midst of the fire, of the cloud, and of the thick darkness, with a great voice: and *he added no more* [italics added]." There is a perfection in the Ten Commandments and in Jesus Christ who uniquely was able to fulfil them. In Jesus Christ we are freed from the inevitable condemnation of the law. Now we live instead by his Spirit. Any man-made code is anticlimatic and spurious.

There is a great temptation for all of us to feel that we shall somehow promote our growth in Christ by submitting to the legalistic code of our particular culture. This is a perilous course. Our true nurture comes from Christ himself and the channels of his grace that have been discussed at length in this book.

Mysticism—Donald Bloesch traces two types of spirituality in church history: the mystical and the evangelical.[4] The former has been dominant in Roman Catholicism and Eastern Orthodoxy. These are broad outlines, of course, for there are streams of mysticism in Protestantism and strong evangelical and biblical emphases in the long history of Catholicism.

Besides being centered on a direct or immediate experience of transcendent reality, mystical religion regards this experience as an encounter with mystery that cannot be expressed in words. According to the anonymous author of *The Cloud of Unknowing*, one of the classics of mystical devotional literature, the mind becomes intellectually blank in contemplation.

In much mystical thought grace is seen as a power *infused* into a man by which he is united with the divine. In contrast, it appears to this writer that the Bible's emphasis is on new life in Christ.

Mysticism is essentially esoteric. It stresses experiences with deity not shared by everyone. It is individualistic and inward in contrast to the outward thrust of the evangelical emphasis. If we are called to spend time in worshipful contemplation of our Redeemer, we should have the goal of sharing this joy with others.

The early Quakers were mystics since they depended on the "Inner Light" to speak in and through them. This subjective guidance was to many of them as important as Scripture.

"Christian and biblical mysticism usually stresses the personal reality of Christ as compared with the impersonal approach of Hinduism. . . . The union is not one of merging essence which destroys personality, but the biblical one

4. Donald G. Bloesch, "Foundations of Evangelical Spirituality" in *Christian Spirituality East and West*, Chicago, Ill.: The Priory Press, 1968.

of union of human love and will with God. . . . Such mysticism was contemplative, personal and practical: action on the plain followed retreat to the mountain."[5]

The mysticism of the Middle Ages was no doubt a reaction to over-institutionalized religion and reflected a desire for a more personal relationship to God.

It is important to remember thankfully the devotional literature of mysticism. Most of it is centered on the person of Christ, his love for us, and his sacrificial death. Loving personal devotion to Christ will enhance our growth but we must not neglect the role of the Word of God which nourishes this very life in Christ.

Quietism—This is a mystical movement of the seventeenth century which was taught by Miguel de Molinos, a Spanish priest influenced by medieval mysticism, and two French Roman Catholics: Madame Guyon, who was influenced by Molinos' writings and, in turn, produced a number of essays; and François de Salignac de la Mothe Fenelon, a priest. Quietism advocates complete passivity— indeed one's very will is destroyed. One ultimately is completely filled by God himself. Growth in grace is not achieved by any striving or effort on our part. We surrender ourselves to God and he will give us a life of victory over sin. Attainment of this state is a crisis experience, subsequent to conversion, which follows a process of mental prayer aiming at perfect rest in the presence of God.

Later Quietistic views were espoused by a prominent Philadelphia area Quaker, Hannah Whitall Smith, author of *The Christian's Secret of a Happy Life*. She, with her husband, Robert Pearsall Smith, were involved in meetings in Britain that led to the founding of the Keswick Convention in the latter part of the nineteenth century.

Quietistic elements survive today in some of the "deeper

5. C. G. Thorne, Jr., "Mysticism," *The New International Dictionary of the Christian Church*, Grand Rapids: Zondervan, 1974.

life" evangelical literature. In recent years reprints of Madame Guyon's writings are being circulated.

There is a wide variety of Christian literature which seeks to promulgate the way of holiness. Some of it may be pietistic, sentimental, or legalistic. Yet in the strangest places one finds treasures of practical help on Christian growth. The way of the Cross has not been monopolized by any one segment of the church.